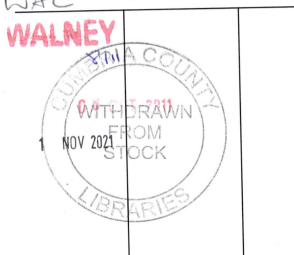
Please return/renew this item by the last due date.
Library items may be renewed by phone on
030 33 33 1234 (24 hours) or via our website

www.cumbria.gov.uk/libraries

Ask for a CLIC password

First edition published 2010
2QT Limited (Publishing)
Burton In Kendal
Cumbria LA6 1NJ

www.2qt.co.uk

Cover Design by Robbie Associates
Cover Photograph by David Reilly
Illustrated Map by Frang McHardy
Typesetting by Dale Rennard
Photographs by Hugh and Margaret Stewart and David Reilly

Printed in Great Britain by
MPG Books Group, Bodmin and King's Lynn

A CIP catalogue record for this book is available
from the British Library

ISBN 978-1-908098-06-1

Hugh Stewart has spent most of his life repairing or replacing bits of folks limbs as an orthopaedic surgeon, for the last twenty years in Lancaster and Kendal. Otherwise walking, climbing, cycling, mountain biking ease the pain, with a special liking for really foul Scottish winter conditions. He first did a long distance walk in 1977, the Coast to Coast, repeated 25 years later, and has devised and walked quite a few since. This is his first attempt at communicating the pleasure they give. He is married and lives near Lancaster.

ACKNOWLEDGEMENTS

I am very grateful to the Ordnance survey for permission to copy their excellent maps.

Without my wife Margaret's original idea, this book would not be here, and I am also grateful to her for shortening my exuberant sentences and other textual corrections. Similarly my father, John, a railway enthusiast, corrected and adjusted the section on the railway.

John Airey of Brookhouse taught me the mysteries of using Word to mark and transfer the maps, many thanks.

Thanks also to Tim and Christine Shaw and David Reilly, who kept good company with us on the original walk, and my son Alistair who accompanied me on a foul December day researching Tebay to Shap. David Reilly's excellent photos also grace some of the pages herein, and there is one of Tony Wragg's also.

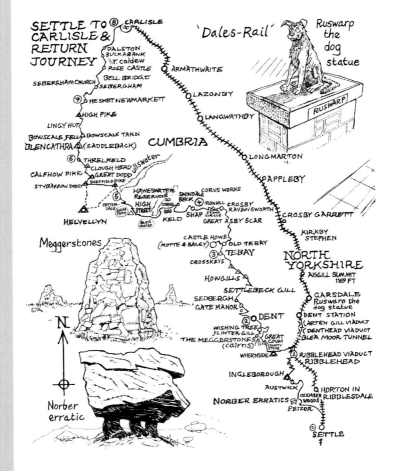

INTRODUCTION

For several years now my wife Margaret and I have gone walking for a week to ten days in Britain in May, allegedly in Spring when the countryside is at its best. These have been a mixture of established walks such as the Coast to Coast and sections of the southwest coastal path, and invented ones in Wales or Scotland.

Towards the end of 2007 we were talking about the possibilities for 2008 when Margaret came up with the idea of walking from Settle to Carlisle and coming back by train, a classic rail journey we had never done. The choice then was between vaguely following the Pennine way and joining up with Hadrian's Wall to get back to Carlisle, or to stride over the Yorkshire hills and the Howgills and over to the Lakes, finishing on the Cumbria Way.

The former necessarily involved some long days over bleak moors, and so the latter was chosen, with most of the days involving ground we knew and loved. The longest day was 15 miles, suitable for our aging limbs, or so I thought until I added up the total ascent.

We planned it for, and did it in, seven days, but were transported from Tebay to Shap; an extra days walking between these two places is included herein for those with more time or blessed with a more obsessive nature, but actually it is a good days walk and the flowers are exceptional, so is recommended, making a round eight days.

This is basically a hill walk with over 22 thousand feet of ascent in 105 miles. **Ingleborough**, **Whernside**, **Great Coum**, **The Calf** and other Howgill tops are taken, then it goes over two little used ridges to **Haweswater Head**, **High Street**, **Sheffield Pike**, the **Dodds**, **Blencathra**, **Bowscale Fell** and **High Pike** of the Northern Fells.

The human settlements visited are interesting and mostly delightful, from the town of Settle, the hamlet of Feizor, villages of Austwick (detour), Horton in Ribblesdale (accommodation), Dent, Sedbergh town, Patterdale, Threlkeld and the little gem of Hesket Newmarket, where we had not set foot before.

Although some of the places are tourist hot spots, not many people visit the Megger stones above Dent; come off the Howgills to Tebay; visit lonely Swindale via the Truss Gap and go over the old corpse road to Haweswater; come off Clough Head to Threlkeld, or visit Bowscale tarn from above.

Hallsfell, Blencathra

THE ROUTE

The route as planned involves some mild scrambling on the penultimate day on Blencathra, although an alternative route can avoid this. It is therefore suitable for virtually any walker who wants to do up to 15 miles a day and be delighted by some of Northern England's best scenery. It also has the virtue of being accessible by train from anywhere in the country.

As it passes through some of England's premier hill walking country, it is not surprising that some of the route will necessarily be on one of the many "Ways" that thread through the area, as the best route from A to B will often be taken by that walk. Rather than try and deviate just for the sake of being unique, which is plainly silly, the "Way" routes are used. They are, in order:

Route	Distance	Description
The Ribble Way:	0.7 miles	Settle to Stackhouse.
The Dales Way:	4.1 miles	Dent to Sedbergh.
The Coast to Coast (reverse):	4 miles	Kidsty Pike to Patterdale.
The Cumbria Way	4.3 miles	Grainsgill Beck Bridge to Nether Row
The Cumbria Way	13.5 miles	All but the first mile of the last day to Carlisle.
Total:	26.6 miles	

MEASUREMENTS

As you can see from the last section, distances are in miles in the text, with metric added for each day's total. Heights are in feet, with occasional metric additions. This is mainly because the measurements of distance and total ascents were made using the Memory Map computer program, which, mine anyway, uses miles and feet. I originally measured distances and calculated ascents from the maps by hand, and then used Memory Map, and determined to use whichever figure was largest. Those using computer generated were always the larger.

Also, despite all the maps now being metric, I was brought up with mile to the inch maps, my car measures distances in miles, speed in mph, fuel usage in mpg: Munro's climbed are by definition in feet. Whilst not wishing to ally myself to such as Mr Clarkson and other 'grumpies', I'm sticking with Alfred Wainwright and miles and feet.

MAP REFERENCES

Where Map references are given, the national grid references are used. This system is explained at the edge of each OS map.

THE WALK

Day 1: Settle to Ribblehead
Distance: 14.5 miles (23 km)   Ascent: 2930 feet
Via: Feizor (café), Norber Scar and its erratic boulders, Ingleborough and its northeast ridge.

Day 2: Ribblehead to Dent
Distance: 10.7 miles (17.2 km)   Ascent: 2360 feet
Via: Bleamoor sidings, Whernside, Great Coum, the Megger stones and Flinter Gill.

Day 3: Dent to Tebay
Distance: 15 miles (24.1 km)   Ascent: 3480 feet
Via: Deeside, Sedbergh and the Howgills.

Day 4 (optional): Tebay to Shap
Distance: 12.6 miles (20.3 km)   Ascent: 1530 feet

Day 5: Shap to Patterdale
Distance: 14.9 miles (23.9 km)   Ascent: 3900 feet
Via: Truss Gap, Swindale, the Old Corpse Road, Mardale, High Street by its East ridge, The Knott and Boredale Hause.

Day 6: Patterdale to Threlkeld
Distance: 10.7 miles (17.2 km)   Ascent: 3580 feet
Via: Glenridding, Sheffield Pike, The Dodds, Clough Head.

Day 7: Threlkeld to Hesket Newmarket
Distance: 11.9 miles (19.1 km)   Ascent: 4167 feet
Via: Blencathra, (Halls Fell), Bowscale Fell and Tarn, High Pike.

Day 8: Hesket Newmarket to Carlisle
Distance: 14.4 miles (23.1 km)   Ascent: 703 feet
Via the Cumbria Way, following the line of the River Caldew.

Total distance: **104.7 miles (168.5 km) Ascent: 22,650 feet.**

SUMMITS

"Wainwrights" and "Birketts" visited en route

A Wainwright is any Fell with a separate chapter in his guide books, marked W; a Birkett is any top mentioned in Bill Birkett's Complete Lakeland Fells, see Further reading, marked B. Where the summits are on alternative routes they are in brackets, and where just off the route they are marked "just off". They are in descending order.

Top	Height (f)	Height (m)	
(Helvellyn)	3118	950	WB
(Lower Man, Helvellyn)	3033	925	B
(Raise)	2896	883	WB
Blencathra	2847	868	WB
(White Side)	2832	863	WB
Great Dodd	2813	857	WB
Atkinson Pike (Blencathra)	2772	845	B
Stybarrow Dodd	2768	843	WB
High Street	2718	828	WB
White Stones (Greenside)	2608	795	B
Watson's Dodd	2588	789	WB
Little Dodd	2575	785	B
The Knott (Just off)	2424	739	WB
Whernside	2415	736	
Clough Head	2381	726	WB
Ingleborough	2373	723	
(Birkhouse Moor)	2356	718	WB
Bowscale Fell	2305	702	WB
Great Coum	2254	687	
The Calf (Howgills)	2220	676	
Sheffield Pike	2215	675	WB
Calders (Howgills)	2211	674	
Calfhow Pike	2175	663	B

High Pike	2157	658	WB
Breaks Head (Howgills)	2070	638	
Rough Crag (High Street)	2060	628	B
Heron Pike (Glenridding)	2008	612	B
Arant Haw (Howgills)	1985	605	
Angletarn Pikes (Just off)	1860	567	WB
Uldale Head (Howgills)	1740	530	
Glenridding Dodd	1450	442	WB

PLANNING THE WALK

Maps

It is recommended that 1:25,000 scale maps be used for the detail. Apart from the last four miles and a mile around Feizor on day 1, only three maps are needed:

OS Explorer OL2, OL19 and OL5.

OS OL 41, and OS 315 complete the set, but small print outs from the Internet will do if you're pushed for weight. In addition, OS OL4 would be needed for the wet weather alternative via Skiddaw House on Day 7.

Luggage transport

For those of you older folk who enjoy a walk unburdened by all the extras for the evenings, like clean clothes, I'm afraid there is no coordinated taxi service such as Sherpa; they only cater for established long distance walks. Some day maybe... They won't even take you on for the one day which is effectively for them the Coast to Coast, Shap to Patterdale!

There are, however, Taxi firms available for the individual days at Settle, Sedbergh, Penrith, Keswick and Carlisle.

Accommodation

This is mentioned here under planning, as there is a potential problem at Ribblehead. There is a good Hotel here, but it is the only accommodation and is at the heart of the three peaks territory and is therefore very busy every weekend.

You can: book very early for the main hotel; use one of their basic bunkhouses; travel by the train of our journey from Ribblehead (17.42 weekdays) to Horton in Ribblesdale, where there are two Hotels, one B&B in the village and another one and a half miles SE of the village, details on the Settle website (www.settle.co.uk). There is also a large campsite. The train to Ribblehead in the morning is at 10am, giving you a leisurely breakfast and wander around, and day two is not a monster anyway. We stayed in Horton.

The Hill Inn at Chapel-le-Dale is an option, but only on weekdays and Sundays, they do not do one night bookings on Fridays or Saturdays.

There is ample accommodation in both Settle and Carlisle, including a YHA hostel and campsite in the latter, but not in Settle, the nearest campsite being at Little Stainforth two miles north. If you had walked from Settle station there you would have done the walk's first mile, and in the morning could join the main route at Feizor for breakfast at the Café, having visited the Celtic wall, see below, en route.

As establishments change I will not list all accommodation, which can be obtained most easily from the Internet.

NOTES ON HILL WALKING

Although an exhilarating activity, especially this walk, hill walking is potentially dangerous. For those new to it let me explain: the weather can turn foul at any time, even on a fine day on setting out, which can lead to you getting lost or cold and wet. Getting lost will at best lead to a long walk out, which in the cold and wet will drain you of energy and make you prone to accidents and possibly worse, i.e. exposure. Folk do die of exposure on English hills! Therefore the minimum you should take on this walk should be:

A - maps as outlined above and a compass.
B - knowledge of how to use them.
C - waterproofs and an extra top layer.

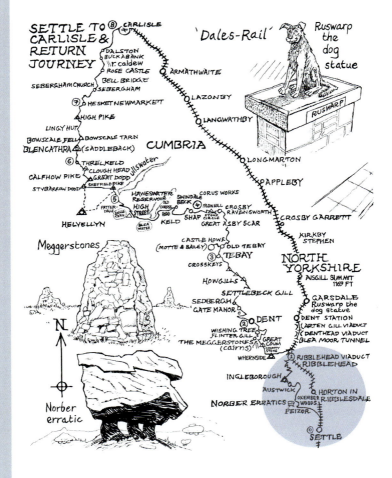

SETTLE TO
CARLISLE &
RETURN
JOURNEY

⑧ CARLISLE

'Dales-Rail'

Ruswarp
the
dog
statue

DALSTON
BUCKABANK
r. caldew
ROSE CASTLE
BELL BRIDGE
SEBERGHAM

ARMATHWAITE

SEBERGHAM CHURCH

RUSWARP

⑦ HESKET NEWMARKET

LAZONBY

HIGH PIKE

LANGWATHBY

LINGY HUT

BOWSCALE FELL   BOWSCALE TARN
BLENCATHRA △ (SADDLEBACK)

CUMBRIA

⑥ THRELKELD
CLOUGH HEAD
CALFHOW PIKE   △ GREAT DODD
STYBARROW DODD   SHEFFIELD PIKE

LONGMARTON

Ullswater

APPLEBY

HAWESWATER
RESERVOIR   SWINDALE   CORUS WORKS
⑤   BECK
HIGH   OLD   ④ IRON HILL
STREET   CORUS   SHAP   CROSBY
KELD   STONE   RAVENSWORTH
CIRCLE
PATTER-
DALE   BLEA
TARN   GREAT ASBY SCAR

CROSBY GARRETT

HELVELLYN

BLEA
WATER

KIRKBY
STEPHEN

Meggerstones

CASTLE HOWE
(MOTTE & BAILEY)   OLD TEBAY
③   TEBAY
CROSSKEYS

NORTH
YORKSHIRE

AISGILL SUMMIT
1169 FT

HOWGILLS

GARSDALE
Ruswarp the
dog statue

SETTLEBECK GILL

DENT STATION

SEDBERGH
GATE MANOR

ARTEN GILL VIADUCT
DENTHEAD VIADUCT
BLEA MOOR TUNNEL

② DENT

N

WISHING TREE
FLINTER GILL
THE MEGGERSTONES
(cairns)

GREAT
COUM
COUNTY
STONE

① RIBBLEHEAD VIADUCT
RIBBLEHEAD

WHERNSIDE

INGLEBOROUGH

Norber
erratic

AUSTWICK

HORTON IN
RIBBLESDALE

NORBER ERRATICS   OXEMBER
WOODS
FEIZOR

⑥ SETTLE

DAY 1
Settle to Ribblehead
**14.5 miles (23 km) 2,930 feet ascent
Via: Feizor (café), Norber Scar and its
erratic boulders, Ingleborough and its northeast ridge.**

Settle

Settle lies where the Craven fault crosses the River Ribble. The Craven fault divides the limestone country to the north and the grit stone hills to the south, and it has created the Aire gap or corridor, a through route from West Yorkshire to Lancaster, the Lakes or Western Dales. "When I were a lad" we travelled this way through Settle before the current bypass, and up over Buck Haw Brow, or 'Booker Brow' as I always thought of it, and on to the Lakes.

Settle from Castlebergh Crag

A turnpike was made here in 1753, the tollbooth being pulled down in 1820 to erect the Town Hall in its place. A bridge across the Ribble was not mentioned until 1498 however. The West Yorkshire to Lancaster railway also used this route, opening in 1847, and this led, of course to the origins of the Settle to Carlisle railway, in 1875, about which later in this guide.

Settle's heyday was in the 17th century, the activities of handloom weaving, stocking knitting and hat making being prominent, and when surprisingly Settle was more important than Bradford or Sheffield! In the late 18th century cotton spinning became the main occupation, with five mills eventually working, powered by the waters of the Ribble.

It describes itself as a "bustling" market town on its website, and it certainly is on Market days, Tuesdays, the market being in the central square.

A good view of the town can be had from the top of Castlebergh crag, a 50 foot limestone cliff recently bolted for the use of climbers. This is accessed by way of Constitution Hill, beside the Shambles. The Shambles is a three storey building overlooking the market square, shops on two levels with houses above. Originally this was a butchers and slaughterhouse in mediaeval times.

A café on the south side of the square bears the name the Naked Man, with a carving and date above the door, which is interesting enough, but their home made cakes cakes and bread alone are worth the visit.

There used to be a museum called charmingly the Pig Yard Club Museum housing remains from the nearby Victoria Cave, but it closed in the 1980s, the relics dispersed to the Leeds and British Museums and to private individuals. The cave was discovered on Queen Vic's accession, hence the name, by a man whose dog disappeared down a foxhole. The current large entrance is man made. The oldest remains were dated at 130,000 years ago, when hyenas probably lived there, dragging bits of hippopotamuses and early rhinoceroses back to feast on. Then successive layers of clay came as glaciers melted, and then about 11,000 years ago, brown bears hibernating, and the earliest evidence of human activity, a reindeer antler harpoon. Roman artefacts completed the top layer.

THE WALK

It should be stated right at the start that if, for any reason, you cannot have, or do not want, breakfast in Settle, then the Feizor Café, some two and a half miles away does a splendid one, and is open from 9.30am seven days a week.

The walk starts on the west side of the Ribble, just over the river bridge taking the main road, the B6480, out of Settle to Giggleswick, SD 816641. It is in tandem with the Ribble Way for the first long half mile, through fields along the Ribble floodplain. It is actually pleasanter right at the start to follow a different path for a short distance, by the river, going round a football pitch and joining the Ribble Way where this goes left at the river. Shortly after the path joins the minor road to Stackhouse, a path leaves the road on the left by the first trees, at a gated stile accessed by steps. This leads through a wood to a field, where you turn left and climb a slope to a stile. The fields are pasture with some naked limestone. Carry on NW across the next field to a gate, after which

Settle - Start of Walk

4

climb left to a dogleg in the wall, follow the left side of the dogleg still heading NW, then go through three fields keeping to the obvious path, until an unenclosed area is reached and you can sail down to Feizor, where a farmhouse café is open every day.

As you approach Feizor, you will see an impressive Limestone cliff to the right, Pot Scar, a popular climbing venue, hence with somewhat polished rock.

As you join the minor road in Feizor, turn right for the splendid café, which is then on your left.

Feeling refreshed, continue westwards on a path just down from the café, signposted, Austwick, which leads through fields with Oxenber Wood on the right. You will see an entry point to the wood as the path passes near it, with an explanatory board.

Approaching Feizor, Oxenber Woods in the distance

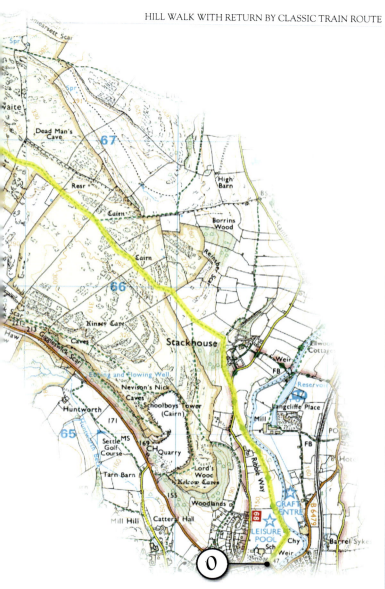

Bloody Cranesbills near Oxenber Woods

The wood is part of Old Woodland Restoration, a project managed by English Nature, and in Spring that is May in these northern climes, it is literally carpeted with woodland flowers.

If an extra 200 feet of climbing and a few hundred yards don't put you off, enter the wood (SD 780680) and go up through the flowers on a walk with red marked posts as a guide. This forks left at a clearing on top, and descends to join a path where turn left and soon join Wood Lane and our route. This diversion is not worth it botanically from midsummer onwards, being a mass of bracken with odd patches of Tormentil.

From the explanatory board rejoin the Austwick path and when it hits a track, turn right and pass Wood House on the track, carrying straight on or actually half left at the junction with Wood Lane, to cross Austwick beck on Flascoe Bridge and join the B road from Austwick. Turn left towards the village and after about 150 yards turn right up Townhead Lane.

The Gate into Oxenber Woods

You will note I have skilfully avoided Austwick, where the devil lurks in the form of a decent pub at lunchtime, the Gamecock. Now there are pubs which have saved my life on walks, namely the Blue Bell at Ingleby Cross on the Coast to Coast, in the days before proper insoles were invented, or possibly known about in my case. Many years ago; it was lunchtime and my feet were wrecked. A worrying amount of alcohol later, worrying to the onlookers that is, the walk to Great Broughton sped by and the feet improved by the day. On the other hand, there have been more pubs which have held the afternoon's walking up so much that darkness has descended before quarters reached, and although wisdom comes with age, some readers may be of the age of temptation.

We preferred to have lunch among the Norber erratics. Those not from these parts will know of Ingleborough, but few will know of the Norber erratics.

Erratics are lumps of rock which shouldn't be where they are, because they were transported by a glacier

A Norber erratic

in the last Ice Age, from half a mile up the valley. They are Silurian slate, dark grey, and rest on Carboniferous limestone, an obvious contrast. Geologically the limestone was laid down on the slate. The main boulder field is above Nappa Scars, and a weird and wonderful sight it is. The softer limestone has eroded around the bases, except where sheltered directly underneath, so they are suspended on their pedestals. Some boulders may rock on the pedestals when, inevitably, you will wish to be photographed on top of one, so be careful, you may be the first to topple one!

Actually, although this is of no use to at all to you on this walk, the best place to view the phenomenon is from higher up and in the evening light, with shadows cast by each boulder.

Then you can see that there are more down below in the first field you cross after leaving the road, except here the bases have been buried by accumulation of soil over centuries.

Back to the route, to get to that field, carry on up Townhead lane, until a couple of hundred yards beyond the last houses where the road is crossed by the track of Thwaite Lane. Turn left here and after about fifty yards turn right, north through the gate or over the stile, heading up the field and eventually following the wall on its left side. Note the half buried erratics as mentioned above.

Note also on your left skyline the fine outline of Robin Proctor Scar, now full of hard bolted climbs, whereas more traditional Yorkshire Limestone climbs are eastwards across the valley on "Crummackdale", marked White Stone on the 1:25,000 map.

At the top of this first field on the left side cross a stile, the gate having been locked for years, and go up past a small cliff on your right. You can now wander upwards to find and traverse the erratic field at will, but I recommend the following route for maximum effect: follow the path round right, parallel to the wall, up some natural limestone steps, and opposite a stile in the wall turn left on a narrow path.

You are now in the erratic field, and eventually you will find a broad green path leading upwards. Leave this obliquely right when you see a high ladder stile in the top right hand side of this field, on another narrow path.

Over the ladder stile you are on the open fell. You can find your own way to the crest of the fell, which is cairned, but for easier progress underfoot and to avoid too much limestone pavement, find the path twenty yards up from the stile, turn right on it and on the next brow you will see a notch on the skyline about half a mile away. Head for this via whichever path suits you, travelling diagonally upwards.

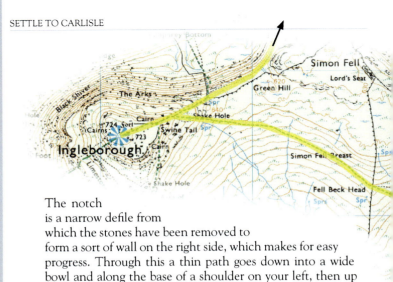

The notch
is a narrow defile from
which the stones have been removed to
form a sort of wall on the right side, which makes for easy
progress. Through this a thin path goes down into a wide
bowl and along the base of a shoulder on your left, then up
and eventually joins the wide path from Clapham to Selside.

The aim now is to locate a small path which cuts the
corner up to Ingleborough, heading for Nick Pot. First
find the junction of three wide paths, the main one you
should be on, the one coming up from Crummack Farm
on the right, and a branch of the path from Clapham
which rejoins from the left. Your shortcut path leaves
the wide green track to Sulber Gate on the left about
170 yards past this junction, and just after a small cairn to the
right of the track where a path coming up on the right from
the valley joins it. This latter path is unmarked on the 2002
Explorer map, but is marked on my downloaded one.

The "shortcut" wends its way between the bare limestone
and joins the main path up from Horton near Nick Pot, an
obvious pothole.

I'm not saying anything about caving, of which there is
obviously an enormous amount of around these parts, as I
know nothing about it and don't really want to. I'm sure it is
fantastically adventurous and a great activity, it just doesn't
appeal to me!

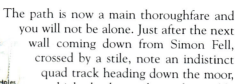

The path is now a main thoroughfare and you will not be alone. Just after the next wall coming down from Simon Fell, crossed by a stile, note an indistinct quad track heading down the moor, which leads easily and quickly down to Gaping Gill. This makes for a pleasant circuit or "racquet" walk of the summit from Clapham, rather than a there and back, for your future reference.

The broad stony path leads gradually upwards until the final steepening, which is now mostly stepped, leading onto the plateau. The summit is further on with a trig point, cairn and cruciate walled shelter. Because there is evidence of huts on the plateau, and ramparts, it is thought that this summit was a fortified village, probably constructed in the first century AD by the Brigantes, against Roman interference. I've often thought about the long distance from water for the poor inhabitants, but there is supposed to be a spring about 50 feet lower than the summit westwards. I've also felt sorry for the inhabitants actually living there, as most times we've visited it whatever season, it's cold, windy and with no visibility. There are some hills like that; Ingleborough may be a good

Ingleborough from the NorthEast ridge

weather hill for others, as Penyghent is for us, but not Ingleborough, it's usually foul on top. The tone was set on the first ascent in the '70s, when we set off one glorious summer's late afternoon with another couple from West Yorkshire, walking up from Ingleton to the summit, which was with no visibility although not actually raining. Map, yes; compass, no.

We wanted to get to the Hill Inn at Chapel-le-Dale, so took direction from the trig point compass directly to the road and just crashed down. There are a few craggy things to negotiate and I couldn't recommend it as a route, but we were young, and learned a lesson: don't leave your wives in a pub while you run back for the car, they'll get chatted up. And always take a compass up on the hills.

You will have noticed a change in vegetation and rock around the wall coming south from Simon Fell, limestone giving way to shale and sandstone, with peat on top giving a moorland setting. The summit plinth is millstone grit.

Primroses and Orchids at Colt Park

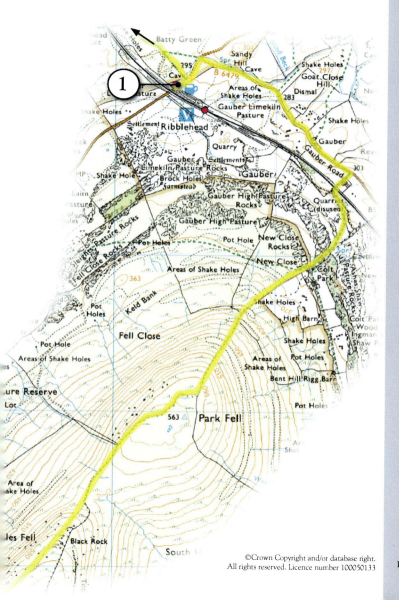

The route to Ribblehead retraces its steps, literally, off the summit but keeps on in the same east-north-east direction when meeting the path up from Horton on which you arrived. This descends further, and when the main path to Chapel-le-Dale descends north, keep going round the great curved rim of Simon Fell on a good path, descending the north ridge of Simon Fell to a broad col, then ascending slightly Park Fell. On meeting a wall on the far side of Park Fell, turn left, still on a definite path, and descend finally to Colt Park, back in Limestone country again and many typical flowers of that habitat.

Just past a wood on the right take the path to the left which leads to a bridge over the railway of our walk, and past Salt Lake cottages, a row of ex-Midland Railway houses built on the site of an old navvy camp of that name to house some of the workers for our railway construction. Salt Lake City in Utah had been founded as a Mormon city and was obviously flavour of the month in the late 1860s.

At the B road turn left and I'm afraid the last bit is on the road, but you can look forward to a drink in the Station Inn, hopefully two if there is enough time before the 1742 train back to Horton if your accommodation is there. While waiting for the train south, look at the northbound platform and wonder that from 1975 to 1993 it did not exist, having been taken out by BR to make new sidings for their ballast quarry.

Notes on The Celtic Wall

This isolated and well preserved wall of some mystery, measuring over twenty yards long by five feet high and wide, can be visited by those who camped at Little Stainforth, as it is just south of the path from there to Feizor on a small escarpment, opposite Smearsett Scar, SD 801674. It is not marked on the ordnance survey maps, which may partially explain why it is still there after what is thought to be over two thousand years. I hope this note doesn't alter that, although a dedicated walk to the wall by Wainwright has not done so. Wainwright wrote that it was thought to be a defence for the encampment in the valley.

NOTES

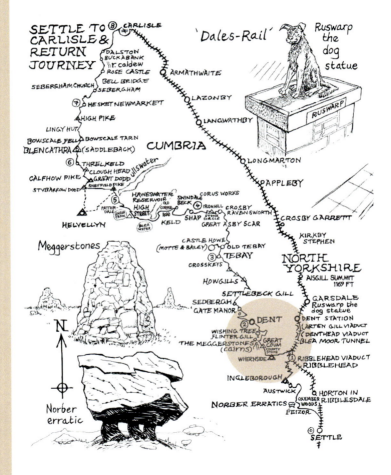

SETTLE TO (8) CARLISLE
CARLISLE & RETURN JOURNEY

DALSTON
BUCKABANK
r. caldew
ROSE CASTLE
BELL BRIDGE
SEBERGHAM
SEBERGHAM CHURCH
(7) HESKET NEWMARKET
HIGH PIKE
LINGY HUT
BOWSCALE FELL BOWSCALE TARN
BLENCATHRA (SADDLEBACK)
(6) THRELKELD
CALFHOW PIKE CLOUGH HEAD
GREAT DODD
STYBARROW DODD SHEFFIELD PIKE
HAWESWATER RESERVOIR
PATTER-DALE HIGH STREET
(5) CORPSE ROAD
BLEA WATER
HELVELLYN

Meggerstones

N

Norber erratic

'Dales-Rail'

Ruswarp the dog statue

RUSWARP

ARMATHWAITE

LAZONBY

LANGWATHBY

CUMBRIA

LONGMARTON

APPLEBY

CORUS WORKS
SWINDALE BECK
(4) IRONHILL
CROSBY RAVENSWORTH
OLD CORPSE ROAD
SHAP STONE CIRCLE
KELD
GREAT ASBY SCAR

CROSBY GARRETT

KIRKBY STEPHEN

CASTLE HOWE
(MOTTE & BAILEY) OLD TEBAY
TEBAY
CROSSKEYS

NORTH YORKSHIRE

AISGILL SUMMIT
1169 FT

HOWGILLS

SETTLEBECK GILL

SEDBERGH
GATE MANOR

(2) DENT
WISHING TREE
FLINTER GILL
THE MEGGERSTONES (CAIRNS)
GREAT COUN COUNTY STONE
WHERNSIDE

GARSDALE
Ruswarp the dog statue
DENT STATION
ARTEN GILL VIADUCT
DENTHEAD VIADUCT
BLEA MOOR TUNNEL

RIBBLEHEAD VIADUCT
RIBBLEHEAD

INGLEBOROUGH

AUSTWICK
NORBER ERRATICS OXENBER WOODS
FEIZOR

HORTON IN RIBBLESDALE

(6) SETTLE

DAY 2
Ribblehead to Dent

**Distance: 10.7 miles (17.2 km) Ascent: 2360 feet
Via: Bleamoor sidings, Whernside, Great Coum, the
Megger Stones and Flinter Gill.**

The ascent of Whernside travels alongside the railway of our walk for a mile and a half or so and then deviates from the easy angled motorway up the hill to give a bit more interest and solitude. If it's poor visibility due to driving rain, or if you want the easiest path underfoot, keep on the main path.

From the Station Inn go downhill over the cattlegrid and take the track on the left that crosses Batty Green. You can go and read the large boards telling you about the "shantytown" here in the 1870s, where 2000 or so men lived while constructing the viaduct, 200 of whom died, but the path carries straight on and up the bank to travel alongside the line. Ponder on the life of those poor souls in winter: there wasn't any Black Sheep then, although alcohol would have been available, the workforce being mainly Irish navvies.

Past Bleamoor sidings, where a loop on the eastern side of the line allows southbound freight trains to be overtaken by passenger trains, the path deviates from the line and crosses some becks and gills, and then the line itself.

*Approaching Ribblehead Viaduct
with Whernside beyond*

DAY 2: RIBBLEHEAD TO DENT

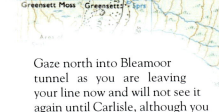

Gaze north into Bleamoor tunnel as you are leaving your line now and will not see it again until Carlisle, although you can see the line in the distance from Whernside and Great Coum.

Clearly the line was not built for the locals, as "Dent" station is four miles from Dent, and the last half mile from the Dee at Cowgill is a strenuous 425 foot ascent, bad enough when descending on a bike, let alone ascending on foot or by bike. The tunnel line is indicated by the airshafts.

The aquaduct on your left carries the Force Gill over the railway: there must have been, I suppose, sound engineering reasons why this was better than merely diverting it alongside the line to join the streams from Greensett Moss, but they're not obvious.

Carry on up the main path until the wall on your left deviates left down to Force Gill and a wire fence continues alongside the path. Cross the fence by the wall over a wooden cross strut and continue on the bank above Force Gill as it curves to the west. After a down and up over a tributary keep to the edge of the high bank overlooking the Gill as it is easier, and cross the Gill where a

Force Gill upper waterfall

wall comes down from the Fell in an easterly direction. Just before this, the second, shyer and sweeter waterfall comes into view.

Note that the small dotted path marked on the 1:25,000 maps as leaving the main highway 250 yards after the wire fence starts does not exist, although you could easily hop over the non-barbed wire fence there.

Follow the wall going up the Fell westwards, first on rough reedy grass and eventually on moorland grass, which starts sooner on the left side, till it curves to the south and you are obviously on Limestone bedrock, when carry on in the same westerly direction across some fragmented pavement.

For those interested in botany, the first deep limestone channel you come across has Mossy Saxifrage on the end wall in spring and summer.

Mossy Saxifrage

20

Carry on upwards in the same line until you come to Greensett Tarn, head for its right (north) end and head obliquely right up the slope, with boggy ground to start with, until the main highway is met again. A gentle wander up the ridge leads to the Trig point. This is not a fantastic summit, but it is the highest of the "three peaks" at 2419 feet or 736 metres, and therefore an achievement if you have not come this way before.

Your descent is almost due west from the trig point, having crossed the wall, on a defined path all the way, and the quickest route to and from the summit from and to a road. It is not on the three peaks route and therefore relatively quiet, although

John Self in his book "The Land of the Lune" suggests that the Loyne three peaks walk, Loyne meaning land of the Lune, should include Great Coum and therefore come this way, going on to Ingleborough, the third peak. Sounds an excellent idea to me.

When limestone is reached again half way down you are likely to see rare flowers such as the mountain scurvy grass, as we did.

On reaching the lonely Dent to Thornton-in-Lonsdale road turn right. You are now more than 1000 feet or 350 metres above Dent, and if you ever want to test your bicycle hill climbing, this ascent from Dent on a gated road seems a good place. You would be glad of the gate for the opportunity of a temporary rest.

After walking down the road for 500 yards or so, turn left up a track, the Occupation Road. This was an old drove road done up for access at the time of the enclosing, or "occupation", of the moorland above Dentdale, but although this was clearly a major and well maintained route in the late 19th century, the bit between Foul Moss and Nun House Outrake (wonderful names) in particular has deteriorated somewhat and is not pleasant going, especially when wet.

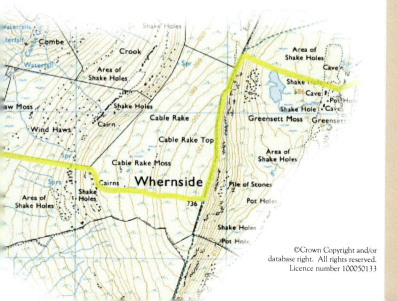

Remember this if you're thinking of shirking the climb to Great Coum, shame on you; once up on the ridge the going is good, particularly coming down, which is springy moss on limestone.

Having found the track again after Foul Moss and turned north, you'll soon see a small wicket stile in a wall a few yards off the track up on the left, which you must pass though to gain access to the boggy hillside. Make obliquely for the col, and do not worry about the wall marked on the map, which will not impede you as it has frequent gaps, and be not afraid, this is open access country.

The county stone is but a large boulder in the wall up from the col, exactly where the wall coming up from Ease Gill on the west side joins the main ridge wall.

County Stone, Great Coum

The wedge of land south-west from here between these two walls is Lancashire, and always has been, whereas before the major boundary changes in 1974 you would now be in the West Riding of Yorkshire, the border of which would follow the current national park boundary round Great Coum and Crag Hill and on to the Lune river, thence north to Carlingill beck which we meet tomorrow. Westmorland would have been "ovver't wall" above Lancashire. Since 1974, the new county of Cumbria has eaten Westmorland, and gorged on this end of the West Riding, now called North Yorkshire, the boundary of which is now over a kilometre south. Not wishing to be considered a victim, the proud old County, God's Own, believes this to be a donation to our poorer neighbours, although the national park men must feel guilty as it all is called the Yorkshire Dales National Park.

Follow the wall, with perhaps a deviation to Gatty Pike cairn for a view; look out for Binks quarry down the East ridge of Great Coum, source of some of the Dent "marble" you'll see on every mantelpiece in Dent. This is a dark limestone containing crinoid fossils, and as it was quarried also at Arten Gill, was used to make the viaducts of our railway there and at Dent Head. After polishing at Stonehouse mill, it also went to decorate various buildings in minor towns such as London and Manchester, but also in Bradford and St Petersburg, where the Tsar had it for his fireplace in 1843.

Stile Gate descending Great Coum

The next side wall is passed through a gap, but the one after has a poor stile which you have to ascend, looking enviously at the better one on the left in old Westmorland. You can shuffle on top to the left to descend the superior version, or boldly find a way down direct. The wall turns westerly here and the final wall separating you from the summit cairn has a stile. The view is extensive, note the Lune valley and some of Morecambe Bay to the South West, the Lakeland skyline, the Howgills of tomorrow, the full length of Dentdale but Dent is hidden.

Turn 90 degrees right at the cairn and head on a thin path just north of east towards the wall you last crossed, following the west side now down the hill on lovely springy moss on

The Meggerstones, Howgills beyond

Limestone, hence the shakeholes evident, over the next wall at a wicket gate stile, follow the path left at the next joining wall and on in the same northerly line till the first Megger Stone is seen, followed by the rest. There is no apparent reason for these monuments, other than there is a lot of loose limestone here ideal for building cairns. And a lovely view of Dent lies below. We had walked around Dent for nearly twenty years and never noticed these stones, but once we knew where they were it's surprising how visible they now were from all over the area.

The quickest way to join the "Ocky" again involves climbing a gate at SD 705854, which the farmer has effectively blocked by placing a large rock in front of it.

To get there you would aim for where the wall to your left has a dog-leg towards you and continues down north-eastwards.

However, as you are good walkers and never ever climb gates in case you damage them, you will have to head to the right, eastwards, picking your way between runnels as you descend. Eventually a quad track appears heading rightwards towards an obvious gate at SD 707851, to join the occupation road once more. Turn left, finding with relief that the surface has now improved.

Just over three quarters of a mile of the "Ocky" brings you to the right turn of Flintergill. Two hundred yards down here, just before a gate, a diagonal path on the left leads up to a viewpoint with a toposcope, which interestingly points out

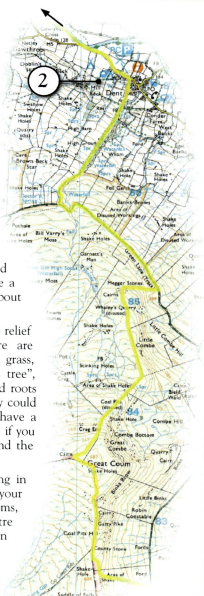

Penyghent, which is hidden by Whernside, but does not mention your fabulous new friends the Megger Stones, which you can see from here and many other places from now on.

Further down it is worth a visit to High Ground Barn, left in a field opposite an old revamped lime-kiln. The barn houses a collection of old farming machinery and implements, but also has a stack of leaflets unless someone has pinched them all that day, which give a lot of useful information about Dent and Flintergill.

Lower down if you want some relief from the stony track, there are some paths on the right on grass, but don't miss the "wishing tree", an old oak with large exposed roots to walk under and wish today could last forever, which will only have a chance of success, apparently, if you go clockwise three times round the root/trunk.

It is worth noting, on arriving in Dent, and before heading for your lodgings or the splendid tearooms, that the Village Heritage Centre shuts at 4pm, and doesn't open till 11am tomorrow!

DENT

A really lovely Dales village with whitewashed houses and a cobbled main street. As the road access is poor from all directions hopefully it will remain relatively unspoilt.

The Dent Brewery may not be the most important subject you are seeking information on, but you're getting it first anyway. Started in 1990 in a barn a couple of miles up the valley, it produces four distinctive bitters, a stout and even a lager. As it owns the George and Dragon you should at least be able to taste them there.

The Wishing Tree, Flinter Gill, Winter

Before or after such tasting, you can't fail to notice the large granite fountain stone, once the only source of drinking water in Dent, opposite the George and Dragon entrance. This is a memorial to Adam Sedgwick, son of the local vicar, born 1785, who went onto Cambridge University and to be a professor of Geology, one of the founders of that subject. He investigated and named the Dent fault, and was involved in the Devonian controversy.

Dent from lower Flinter Gill, Winter

He also studied theology, but upset the church with his forward views on Geology: after one speech in York the entire chapter house refused to sit down with him!

On the other hand, he violently disagreed with Darwin, one of his Cambridge pupils, about evolution and natural selection, championing the Churches' conservative viewpoint. Being a son of Dent, however, he maintained warm relations with Darwin until his death.

The tale of a "vampire", George Hodgson, may sound a bit daft to you modern science-savvy cynics, but perhaps not when you read about the curse of Carlisle later. He died in 1715 aged 94, quite a bit older than his peers, hence the suspicion some other forces were at work, especially as his canine teeth remained his own. When some unexpected deaths occurred, and a "ghost" was seen in the churchyard, there was a general outcry and he was exhumed, brought close to the church porch and reburied with a stake through his heart, the hole in the gravestone being there for all to see!

Look up about the Terrible Knitters of Dent yourselves, I'm off for some Kamikaze (OG 1047, ABV5%).

The Sedgwick Stone, Dent

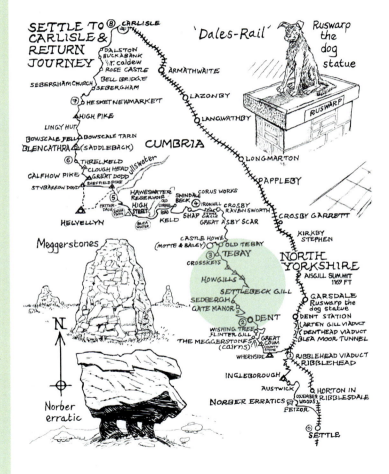

SETTLE TO CARLISLE & RETURN JOURNEY

⑧ CARLISLE

'Dales-Rail'

Ruswarp the dog statue

RUSWARP

DALSTON
BUCKABANK
r. caldew
ROSE CASTLE
BELL BRIDGE
SEBERGHAM
SEBERGHAM CHURCH
⑦ HESKET NEWMARKET
HIGH PIKE
LINGY HUT
BOWSCALE FELL   BOWSCALE TARN
BLENCATHRA (SADDLEBACK)
⑥ THRELKELD
CALFHOW PIKE   CLOUGH HEAD
GREAT DODD
STYBARROW DODD   SHEFFIELD PIKE
PATTER-DALE
HELVELLYN
⑤ HAWESWATER RESERVOIR
HIGH STREET
KELD
BLEA WATER
OLD CORPSE ROAD
SHINDALE BECK
④ IRONHILL
STONE CIRCLE
SHAP CIRCLE
GREAT ASBY SCAR
CORUS WORKS
CROSBY RAVENSWORTH

ARMATHWAITE
LAZONBY
LANGWATHBY
CUMBRIA
LONG MARTON
APPLEBY
CROSBY GARRETT
KIRKBY STEPHEN
NORTH YORKSHIRE
AISGILL SUMMIT 1169 FT
GARSDALE
Ruswarp the dog statue
DENT STATION
ARTEN GILL VIADUCT
DENTHEAD VIADUCT
BLEA MOOR TUNNEL
① RIBBLEHEAD VIADUCT
RIBBLEHEAD
HORTON IN RIBBLESDALE
FEIZOR
© SETTLE

Meggerstones

CASTLE HOWE (MOTTE & BAILEY)
OLD TEBAY
③ TEBAY
CROSSKEYS
HOWGILLS
SETTLEBECK GILL
SEDBERGH
GATE MANOR
② DENT
WISHING TREE
FLINTER GILL
THE MEGGERSTONES (cairns)
GREAT COUM
COUNTY STONE
WHERNSIDE
INGLEBOROUGH
AUSTWICK
NORBER ERRATICS
OXENBER WOODS

N

Norber erratic

DAY 3
Dent to Tebay

**Distance: 15 miles (24.1 km)   Ascent: 3480 feet
Via: Deeside, Sedbergh and the Howgills.**

From Dent to Millthrop you will be following the Dales Way for the first few miles, alongside the delightful Dee. To get to it either take the Ribblehead/Hawes road Northeast from the centre of the village to Church Bridge, which gives a longer riverside walk, or leave via the Sedbergh road and quit it where it deviates from the river after 500 yards.

The meadows are a delight in spring as they are full of flowers, but there are a good many of them, with gates, stiles, mini bridges over streams etc to negotiate. Just before two miles the path joins the quiet back lane to Sedbergh, continuing on this for just over a mile to Brackensgill where turn north up a track. The map shows a ford crossing the Dee but don't fret, there is a footbridge just downstream of the ford.

The track leads upto the Dent to Sedbergh road, where turn left and then almost immediately right up a signposted track by an interesting door in the wall. The track leads up and along the side of a low fell, Long Rigg. Follow the Dales Way round the spur of Long Rigg, where the Howgill Fells are well seen.

Crossing the Dee near Brackensgill; you may use the bridge

Back Gateway into Gate Manor, on the Path from Dent to Sedbergh Road.

THE HOWGILLS

It is surprising how little the average hill walker of northern Lancashire and Cumbria knows of these steep-sided, round-domed grassy hills, which enjoy splendid views and are relatively lonely compared with the Lakes and the Dales to either side. The walking is easy on the tops, and for all the above reasons is superb.

North of the Calf, however, the ridge path is not made up (it is from Calders to the Calf), and careful map reading is required in bad visibility, as it all looks the same.

Their base rock is Silurian sandstone, but this is rarely seen, except at Cautley Crag on the East side, where there is nothing for the climber, except ice climbing in exceptional winters like 2010, and at Black Force, where there is some scrambling to be had. You could visit Black Force on the walk via a slight deviation but if you do it for the scrambling it is like all scrambles, much better up than down and the route is down. Recently there has been an access ban on Black

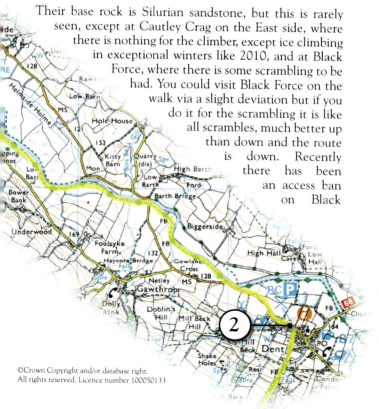

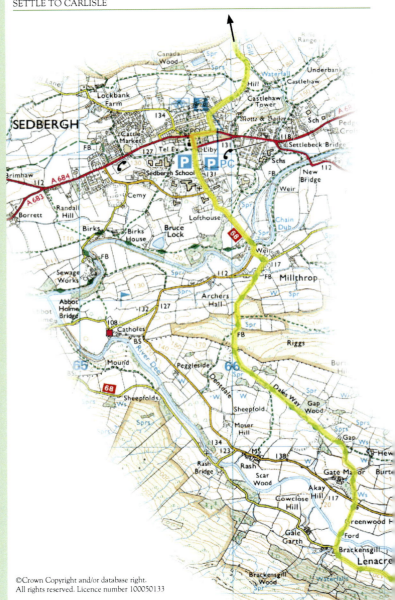

Force and the grassy rib to its east side, due to raptors nesting, between mid February and the end of June. Check with the British Mountaineering Council on their website. Further scrambling would be involved along the Carlingill to return to the route, especially at

The Howgills from the South

the Spout waterfall, where a deviation north up the steep hillside would be necessary unless you are brave and talented.

Back with the walk, follow the Dales Way down to a minor Road at Millthrop. Keep on this road in the same direction for about a hundred yards and turn left on a further road to join the Main Road into Sedbergh, crossing the Rawthey, another tributary of the Lune, on a fine bridge.

There is a footpath on the right a couple of hundred yards up the road which leads to the east end of the town centre, but it is more interesting on this occasion, to walk up the road admiring the fine Sedbergh School playing fields on the left and then the School itself. You join the main Street at the top, turn right for the shops, including teashops. Back Lane, see below, is a right turn past the Loftus Hill car park, to view Railton Yard spinning gallery.

Sedbergh School sports ground

SEDBERGH

From the Norse sett burgh, flat-topped hill, thus really naming the Howgills. Sedbergh is a fine old Market Town, historically part of the West Riding of Yorkshire, hence it used to be said that if the wealthy of Bradford, particularly, could not get their lads into the Grammar School there, Sedbergh School was the next choice. Nowadays I'm sure that is not the case, and the school is co-educational. Founded in 1525, the school became a grammar school in 1551, and independent in 1875. It now tends to dominate the town.

The town grew as a centre of farming, wool production, weaving and knitting, situated as a natural centre where the Rawthey, Dee and Clough(Garsdale) rivers join and meet the Lune a little further west. You can see what a spinning gallery looked like in the 18th century in Railton Yard, just off Back Lane.

Sedbergh is now England's designated, indeed only, book town, Hay-on–Wye being in Wales of course. Mostly. Whereas Hay has been a book town for many years, Sedbergh only became one in 2003 as a result of the Foot and Mouth outbreak of 2001, the idea being to re-attract tourism. There are six bookshops and a festival of Books and Drama in September.

Having perhaps bought a book or two, you have a choice of a direct route up the Howgills or a minor deviation to view a small but well formed motte and bailey castle, Castlehaw

Tower. This is in a wooded situation with a good view of the town, and is a much better monument, with an information board e.g. than tomorrows' castle at Tebay.

Approaching Settlebeck Gill and the Howgills

The direct route proceeds north up Joss Lane, which is off Main Street by the car park, veering right by the Outdoor shop and onto a track past a gate at the end of the tarmac. Fork left soon after the gate and head upto the fells alongside Settlebeck Gill, passing a wicket gate, stile, and kissing gate before gaining the Access area.

To view Castlehaw Tower, go east down Main Street to where Back Lane joins it, and turn left in front of Westwood Books up a track. This leads round right and a gate on the right leads into the site.

This was a Norman Castle built of wood against Scottish attacks. I can't imagine it would have withstood a determined attack from an army with matches! It is certainly a fine vantage point, however, and was used by the Royal Observer Corps in the last war, and in the '60s an underground bunker against nuclear attack was dug in to the bailey, although most of Sedbergh would have been disappointed.

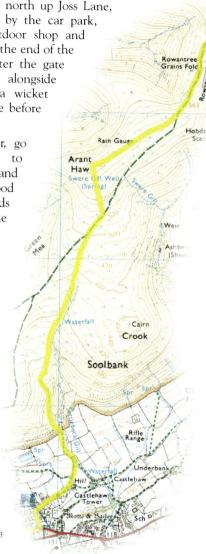

Back on the track, almost opposite the gate to the site, another gate leads north up a field to the right of Hill Farm, to join the path from Hill Farm alongside Settlebeck Gill.

Here there is a choice of a zig-zag path to the left or a steeper one straight on. They join to head north to eventually join the main path from Winder, which used to be climbed many times by every Sedbergh pupil. I wonder if things have changed? On the way up notice the path to Arant Haw you can see peeking through the gap ahead. Shortly after joining the main path, it divides; the left hand branch rising with surprising steepness to the summit of Arant Haw, this being the path you saw on the way up, whilst the right branch goes more gently round the summit but only ascends a few feet less.

We once spotted two Sedbergh pupils on the steeper path stopping to examine the path every ten yards or so. On questioning they were measuring the erosion of the path for a project. I should have asked how they could do that, as the path is not exactly inset into the hill. Ask the next one you see!

From Arant Haw you see the Lakeland hills in the west, with the Scafell/Scafell pikes notch prominent; ahead is the main Howgill chain with the western ridges running down to the

Lune valley; northeast is the characteristic outline of Wild Boar Fell; further round east the mass of Baugh Fell, oft not visited; then the three peaks, with Whernside the amorphous mass in the middle; then Great Coum, yesterday's last summit.

Curious water channels on the Howgills

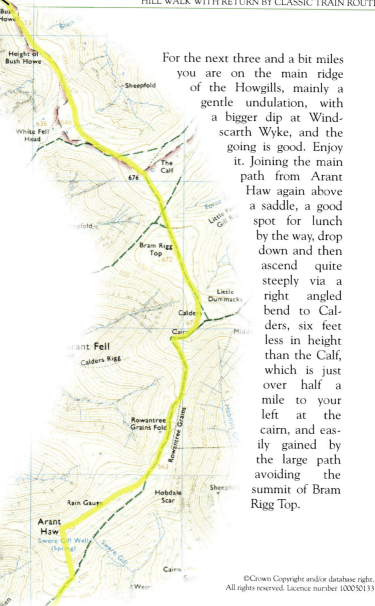

For the next three and a bit miles you are on the main ridge of the Howgills, mainly a gentle undulation, with a bigger dip at Windscarth Wyke, and the going is good. Enjoy it. Joining the main path from Arant Haw again above a saddle, a good spot for lunch by the way, drop down and then ascend quite steeply via a right angled bend to Calders, six feet less in height than the Calf, which is just over half a mile to your left at the cairn, and easily gained by the large path avoiding the summit of Bram Rigg Top.

38

The Calf is the highest fell of the Howgills, at 2220 feet or 676 metres for the younger readers. You can't miss the summit as there is an Ordnance Survey column right on the path. The views are extensive, the Lakeland peaks are to the west from the Coniston Fells right round to Blencathra, which is three days away, and you should be able to make out the flat top of High Street, which is due the day after tomorrow, just to the right of Helvellyn and the pimple of Catstyecam. Wainwight's "Walks on the Howgill Fells" gives an excellent view diagram from here.

Continue northwesterly on your high level traverse to White Fell head, the path actually skirts the summit, and swing round to the north bound for the Height of Bush Howe.

There is a "Horse" shape on the southwestern slopes of this fell, the Horse of Busha, which you will not see from the main path. It is a natural shape of stones on the grassy fellside, and not named on the maps.

From Bush Howe there is a dip to Windscarth Wyke and a climb to Breaks Head, where we leave the spine of these hills and descend. First go West on a path, and when it starts to swing to the south leave it in a north westerly direction for the pathless grassy ridge called Ulgill Rigg., which descend heading for where Great Ulgill beck changes course from northwest to west, to cross this and on to the Blakethwaite Stone.

If you wish to view the aforementioned Black Force, a series of waterfalls, leave the ridge to the left and follow the Little Ulgill

Howgills from the Lune Valley, January

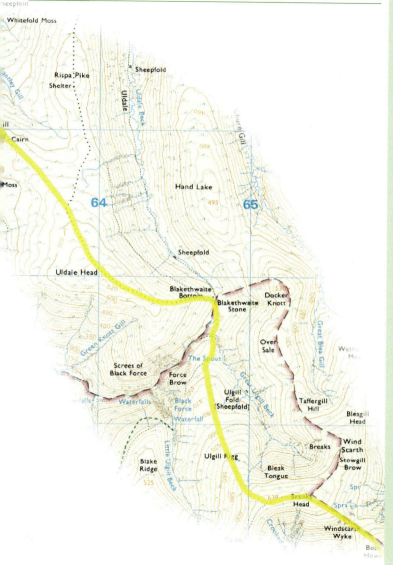

Whitefold Moss

Rispa Pike
Shelter

Sheepfold

Uldale

Uldale Beck

Church Gill

Cairn

Moss

Hand Lake

495

64

65

Sheepfold

Uldale Head

Blakethwaite
Bottom

Blakethwaite
Stone

Docker
Knott

Over
Sale

Great Blea Gill

Wetha
Mo

Green Knott Gill

The Spout

Screes of
Black Force

Force
Brow

Great Ulgill Beck

Ulgill
Fold
(Sheepfold)

Taffergill
Hill

Bleagill
Head

Waterfalls

Waterfalls

Black
Force
Waterfall

Breaks

Wind
Scarth
Stowgill
Brow

Little Ulgill Beck

Blake
Ridge

Ulgill Rigg

Bleak
Tongue

525

638

Breaks
Head

Windscarth
Wyke

Crooked

Cairn

Sprs

Bus
How

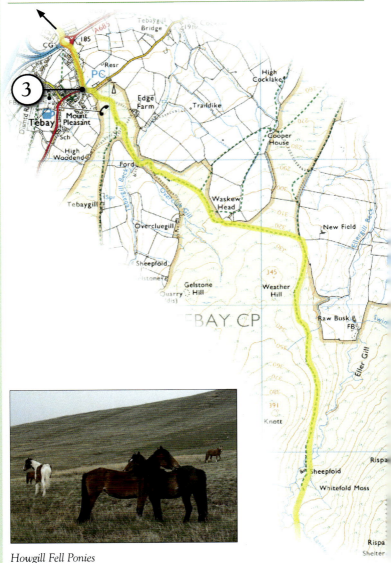

Howgill Fell Ponies

Beck till it becomes Black Force. The descent here is very steep alongside the Force, and when you get to the bottom you have to scramble right along the Carlingill and either avoid the Spout, a 30 foot waterfall, by a scramble to the left or take a path on the steep hillside which may not be to everybody's liking. See above about potential access restrictions here.

It has to be said that the Blakethwaite Stone is not exactly a fabulous monolith. In fact the first time we came here it took a while to find it in the vegetation. It is the second stone you come to on the path through to Uldale, and twenty yards or so beyond the path leading leftwards up Uldale head, which is our route.

From the top of Uldale head the aim is to join the path marked on the 1:25,000 map a mile north-north-west, by a sheepfold. There is no path so you will have to pick your own route, the only part of this walk where you are on your own, so enjoy it. This is the real empty quarter of the whole walk, if you see anyone here they have either been given a copy of this guide free and therefore must be a friend or relative, or, especially if old and wild looking, may approach you to see if World War two has ceased. Both types are highly dangerous, and if spotted it is advised to pretend to be a tussock until they've wandered off!

You may see here, however, as we did, the semi-wild fell ponies. Semi-wild, because they were being rounded up by two locals on quadbikes, just to the east of the path beyond the sheepfold, for reasons unknown.

It is a little tussocky, but once on the path you romp northwards, turning westwards after you've come alongside a wall on your right and that is joined by a wall on its right at a right angle. This leads past the scruffy Waskew Head and down to a ford, up to join a track and down to Tebay. The Cross Keys is 200 yards left along the main road to Kendal if a drink is desired. If?

Sheepfo

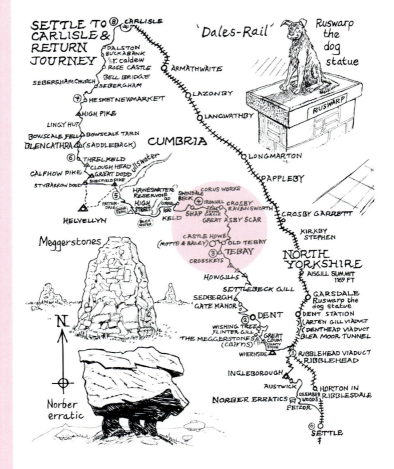

SETTLE TO CARLISLE & RETURN JOURNEY

'Dales-Rail'

Ruswarp the dog statue

⑧ CARLISLE

DALSTON
BUCKABANK
r. caldew
ROSE CASTLE
BELL BRIDGE
SEBERGHAM
SEBERGHAM CHURCH
⑦ HESKET NEWMARKET
HIGH PIKE
LINGY HUT
BOWSCALE FELL   BOWSCALE TARN
BLENCATHRA (SADDLEBACK)
⑥ THRELKELD
CLOUGH HEAD
CALFHOW PIKE   GREAT DODD
STYBARROW DODD   SHEFFIELD PIKE
⑤ HAWESWATER RESERVOIR
PATTERDALE   HIGH STREET
HELVELLYN   GOOSE TARN   BLEA WATER   KELD

ARMATHWAITE
LAZONBY
LANGWATHBY

CUMBRIA

LONGMARTON
APPLEBY

SWINDALE BECK   CORUS WORKS
OLD CORPSE ROAD   ④ IRONHILL   CROSBY RAVENSWORTH
SHAP   STONE CIRCLE   GREAT ASBY SCAR

CROSBY GARRETT

KIRKBY STEPHEN

Meggerstones

CASTLE HOWE (MOTTE & BAILEY)   OLD TEBAY
③ TEBAY
CROSSKEYS

NORTH YORKSHIRE

AISGILL SUMMIT 1169 FT

HOWGILLS

SETTLEBECK GILL

N

SEDBERGH
GATE MANOR   ② DENT
WISHING TREE
FLINTER GILL
THE MEGGERSTONES (cairns)
WHERNSIDE   GREAT COUM   COUNTY STONE

GARSDALE
Ruswarp the dog statue
DENT STATION
ARTEN GILL VIADUCT
DENTHEAD VIADUCT
BLEA MOOR TUNNEL

① RIBBLEHEAD VIADUCT
RIBBLEHEAD

INGLEBOROUGH

AUSTWICK   ⑩ HORTON IN RIBBLESDALE
NORBER ERRATICS   OXENBER WOODS
FEIZOR

Norber erratic

SETTLE

DAY 4
Tebay to Shap
12.6 Miles (including Castle Howe)
20.3 km, 1530 ft ascent.

Tebay grew in importance when the railway from Lancaster to Carlisle was built in the 1840s, to open up travel to Scotland, and is therefore tied in with the history of our line, which see later on. It became a major railway town serving the main line over Shap Summit, but unfortunately was stripped by nice Dr Beeching in 1968. The motorway and its various services are its main employer now, the services on the M6 being the only national ones built and run by locals, and I can fully recommend the farm shop if you return this way by car.

Castle Howe

The route includes a visit to this Motte and Bailey Castle by the Lune, although it is merely a bare earthwork with no placards etc. If you are imaginative and romantic it is worth a visit.

From the large roundabout take the road to Old Tebay until it veers away from the noisy M6, where a footpath sign by a gate on the left indicates a track leading north a short way, through another gate and back under the M6. A small beck crosses in front of the earthwork so keep alongside the M6 fence south till a small bridge crosses it.

The castle, presumably built to defend the obvious route south through the Lune gap, is undated but it is known that in the 12th century was the home of a Mr De Tibbay.

The Motte is now crescent shaped, most obvious when climbed from the gap twixt it and the bailey, rather than round as it once was, more likely to be due to the action of the Lune rather than that of the local people.

44

Back on the road to Orton, after a hundred yards a public bridleway is marked on the right, ungated, turning into a green lane. At a gate the green lane looks as if it becomes a bit overgrown in summer, so either use an animal track in the field to the right or go direct to the A685 by a marked footpath. If continuing forward by lane or field, the triangular field ends at a gate leading to the main road, but by now a decent track leads to a footpath sign at the main road further on.

Cross the road, careful as although not very busy this means some cars are near terminal velocity, through a gate at a public bridleway sign. This leads to a ford, which we couldn't cross after heavy rain, the road bridge edge helping out. A stile at the far side leads to field, where keep parallel to the road to a gap in the first wall, then a gate in the next, then turn half right to a stile and wooden bridge. Head up the slope to the right, heading to the right of the houses at Row End, where a stile gains you the road to Gaisgill. Just past Row End a gate on the left with a footpath sign leads down a field in which, if it were not for the driving rain you could imagine you were in Peru when a Llama comes to lick any of your exposed anatomy. Don't worry, it's in an enclosure.

You're probably thinking this is a tad bitty and broken by these stiles and closed gates, but the alternative is the road, so press on and look north to the limestone uplands in a few miles, where the walking is glorious and no stiles hinder you till after Crosby Ravensworth!

Common Spotted Orchids, Knott Lane

At the bottom a double stile leads down a steep bank to recross the main road. Turn right for 50 yards, and left over a stile into a field where turn half-right down to the Lune, cross a side steam and through a gate by the river. Follow this round to join the B6261 at a gate, left over the Lune and take the second signed footpath on the left through a gate, immediately up the slope on the right and over the remains of a Tumulus. A stile just to the left of a gate on the left of the farm leads to a field which you climb heading for a gate in a fence at the top. Through this notice a yellow marker on a tree to your left indicates the way, alongside the wall which leads to a hidden stile round a turn in the wall.

Turn right on the minor road to Raisbeck, crossing a B road, and after six hundred yards or so a signed footpath on the left at a gate leads you by a wall then a fence and through an open gate on the right. Just before the gap in the next wall a blue sign indicates the way

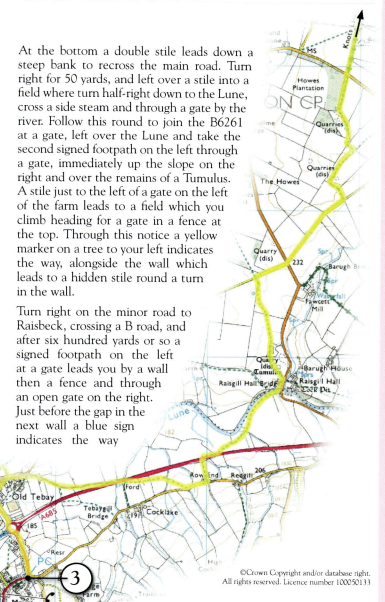

along the wall to the left. Note that if the ground so far today has been very boggy, it would be advisable to carry straight on here to join the B road at New House and join the route later, as the last bit of our route before that road will be the boggiest yet.

If dry, at the top of the wall signed by blue is a gate on the right, go through this and by some sheep pens to reach an open field go through a gate immediately on your left, through a wall and follow this across a grassy quarried moonscape, curving right down a wide walled channel through a boggy region where we saw snipe, and through a gate to freedom.

Straight ahead up the public byway which is a botanist's paradise in spring and summer, noticing the crossing of the Coast to Coast walk before crossing another gate and into open access land, Great Asby Scar. A track or path now leads across this and the walking is easy, allowing you to stride off and enjoy the views at last.

A signed enclosed feature is a mirage unfortunately, the reality being a covered reservoir with solar panels.

Keep on upwards and along until you see a gate in the top left hand corner of the hollow you curve round, go through this and continue up to the top of the hill. You will see a wall on the left coming from the west and then angling north-east. Follow the track which leads towards a gate in the wall a short distance north from the angle, and go through it. A small path now leads exactly north, heading for a post where the path joins a track from the left which is not marked on the maps, although the continuation is, which soon crosses a metalled track leading to an obvious quarry.

Great Asby Scar

If it were not for the limestone, the moorland setting could be Dartmoor, the good path gently undulating across the plateau with big views.

Crosby Ravensworth

You spy a road off to the left which dips and turns to the left, and your path joins the road at this bend, where carry on northerly till a public byway sign on the crest of the next hill on the left points you along and then down, joining a minor road and down the side of the lovely Lyvennet beck valley.

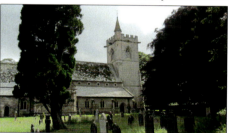

St Lawrence's Church, Crosby Ravensworth

Near the bottom a green lane on the left appears with a public way sign leading down to a bridge across the Lyvennet, then leading to a small road, turn left here and up to the main street of Crosby Ravensworth by St Lawrence's church.

The church dates from early 12th century, with a major overhaul and some more additions in the 19th century. A cross shaft dating from the 7th century is in the churchyard. At the time of our visit the Grade 1 listed building was for sale for "recreational or educational use"!

Turn left if not visiting the church, or use the path on the far side of another beck, Dalebanks, if visiting. Watch out for Monkey Flowers in the beck in summer. Either way the route is then right up the B Road to Shap marked three and a half miles distant. So near!

When we passed through, the Butchers Arms tantalisingly appearing through the rain down the Orton road was closed and for sale, but has opened since, you may be pleased to hear. A lovely village but with both church and pub for sale it had an air of a ghost town in the making, especially on a dark December Sunday. Let's hope not.

After a couple of bends up the Shap road a public footpath sign to Haber on the left points you down a steep bank, through a wall gap and into a field. Follow the edge of the field upwards through one open gate, and then be careful not to miss a stile near the next gate, which leads rightwards into a triangular field. Keep to the right side along-

Giant Bellflowers, Woods at Haberwain Lane

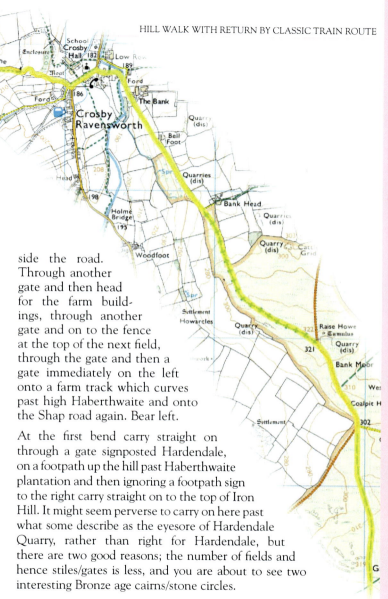

side the road. Through another gate and then head for the farm buildings, through another gate and on to the fence at the top of the next field, through the gate and then a gate immediately on the left onto a farm track which curves past high Haberthwaite and onto the Shap road again. Bear left.

At the first bend carry straight on through a gate signposted Hardendale, on a footpath up the hill past Haberthwaite plantation and then ignoring a footpath sign to the right carry straight on to the top of Iron Hill. It might seem perverse to carry on here past what some describe as the eyesore of Hardendale Quarry, rather than right for Hardendale, but there are two good reasons; the number of fields and hence stiles/gates is less, and you are about to see two interesting Bronze age cairns/stone circles.

Half a Bronze Age Stone Circle, top of Iron Hill with the Pennines in the distance

The first is near the top of the hill, easily missed although it is right on the path. The wall actually bisects the stone circle, the north half of which has been removed. A large skeleton was dug up here in the early 19th century, and a bronze dagger found nearby. The intact cairn stone circle is seventy yards south i.e. left of here.

Suitably impressed, or possibly not, press on, enjoying the view of the huge quarry, actually a lake on our trip, in a few more years of global warming winters it will be a boating lake. I wonder if the wet weather of late 2009 has disrupted the quarry workings.

The path becomes a wide green lane and then a road, which after a cattle grid turns to the right but you press on straight ahead on a signed public footpath which curves round the quarry fence climbing to head for a what appears to be a gate at the top on the right between a wall and a fence, but actually a wooden stile there gives access to a

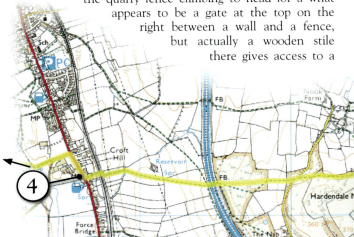

field which you travel west through, keeping to the fence, and do NOT go over the next stile on the right, keep on until you see the minor road, where the path crosses it by wooden signposts one on each side.

Corus Works, Shap, 'Queen Mary', from Hardendale Nab with Wet Sleddale beyond

Go through a gate or a stile to its right and down the field to cross the wall at the bottom by an unobtrusive stone stile marked with some green paint. Over this you are once again in open access land so carry on downwards in the same line until you see the footbridge over the M6, which you cross.

Head approximately 45 degrees after the M6, aiming just to the right of the pylon at the bottom, through a gate at the corner. Carry straight on over the mound, probably all a hidden reservoir, through a gate in the middle of the next wall, where an obvious track leads down to the mainline railway. Ignore the tempting tunnel straight ahead, the path does a dogleg to the right before leading straight to the side of the Greyhound and a welcome drink.

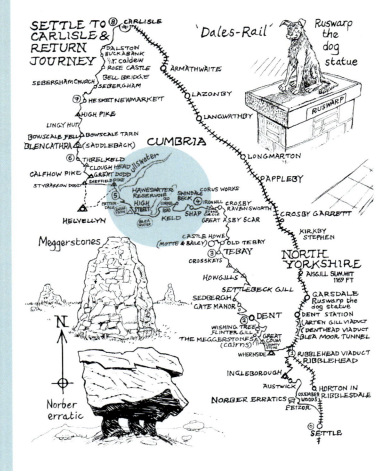

SETTLE TO
CARLISLE &
RETURN
JOURNEY

'Dales-Rail'

Ruswarp
the
dog
statue

CARLISLE ⑧

DALSTON
BUCKABANK
r. caldew
ROSE CASTLE
BELL BRIDGE
SEBERGHAM
SEBERGHAM CHURCH

ARMATHWAITE

LAZONBY

HESKET NEWMARKET ⑦

LANGWATHBY

HIGH PIKE

LINGY HUT

RUSWARP

BOWSCALE FELL   BOWSCALE TARN
BLENCATHRA (SADDLEBACK)

CUMBRIA

THRELKELD ⑥
CLOUGH HEAD
CALFHOW PIKE   GREAT DODD
STYBARROW DODD   SHEFFIELD PIKE

Ullswater

LONGMARTON

APPLEBY

HAWESWATER
RESERVOIR   SWINDALE
BECK   CORUS WORKS

PATTER-
DALE   ⑤   HIGH
STREET   OLD
CORPSE
ROAD   ④ IRONHILL   CROSBY
RAVENSWORTH

CROSBY GARRETT

HELVELLYN   BLEA
WATER   KELD   SHAP   STONE
CIRCLE   GREAT ASBY SCAR

KIRKBY
STEPHEN

Meggerstones   CASTLE HOWE   OLD TEBAY
(MOTTE & BAILEY)   ③ TEBAY

NORTH
YORKSHIRE

CROSSKEYS

AISGILL SUMMIT
1169 FT

HOWGILLS

SETTLEBECK GILL

GARSDALE
Ruswarp the
dog statue

N

SEDBERGH
GATE MANOR   DENT ②

DENT STATION
ARTEN GILL VIADUCT
DENTHEAD VIADUCT
BLEA MOOR TUNNEL

WISHING TREE
FLINTER GILL
THE MEGGERSTONES
(cairns)   GREAT
COUM   COUNTY
STONE

WHERNSIDE   RIBBLEHEAD VIADUCT
RIBBLEHEAD

INGLEBOROUGH

Norber
erratic

AUSTWICK
NORBER ERRATICS   OXENBER
WOODS   FEIZOR

HORTON IN
RIBBLESDALE

SETTLE ⑥

DAY 5
Shap to Patterdale

Distance: 14.9 miles (23.9 km)   Ascent: 3900 feet
Via: Truss Gap, Swindale, the Old Corpse Road,
Mardale, High Street by its East ridge,
The Knott and Boredale Hause

You might think that "Shap to Patterdale" is the reverse of day four (or five) of the Coast to Coast walk, but it's not, and in my humble opinion it's an improvement, exploring lonely Swindale rather than the side of a Reservoir, and particularly coming across the tremendous view of Mardale head on the old Corpse Road. The ridge up High Street is a "connoisseurs route" according to AW himself, better than the way up Kidsty Pike. Obviously you are going to the Lake District, and not away from it, which most will think an improvement, and finally if it's a fine day there is the prospect of a dip in Angletarn in the afternoon. The last four miles is the exact reverse of the Coast to Coast, however.

Shap is a long town, so there are several starting points depending on where you stay, but all of them must join where the minor road crosses the River Lowther, southwest of the hamlet of Keld. I will describe the most southern approach, as if staying at the Greyhound Hotel.

This approach crosses a river by some stepping stones and some marshy ground. If it is very wet or has been, it may be pleasanter to cut out the marshy

Stepping Stones at Thornship

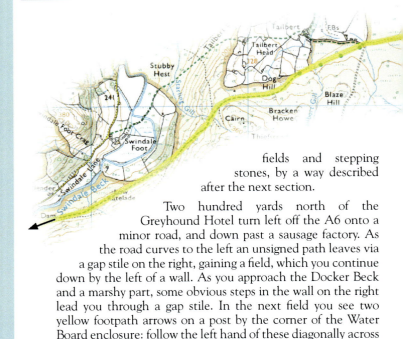

fields and stepping stones, by a way described after the next section.

Two hundred yards north of the Greyhound Hotel turn left off the A6 onto a minor road, and down past a sausage factory. As the road curves to the left an unsigned path leaves via a gap stile on the right, gaining a field, which you continue down by the left of a wall. As you approach the Docker Beck and a marshy part, some obvious steps in the wall on the right lead you through a gap stile. In the next field you see two yellow footpath arrows on a post by the corner of the Water Board enclosure: follow the left hand of these diagonally across this field, which, it has to be said, is very marshy after wet weather so it is best to skirt round the centre of the field to the right, aiming to the right of the obvious gate, as your exit is over another gap stile to the right of the gate. Walk up beside the broken wall towards the left side of the house on the hill, and at the top go right over the remains of the wall and join a lane on the left through an iron gate. Turn right, past the house and turn first left on another enclosed lane, which joins a broader one through a gate, and down to curve round right to Township Farm.

The wet weather route gets to this point by keeping on the minor road past the sausage factory, and taking the second signed footpath "Township" on the right, over a gap stile and down to an obvious footbridge. The path carries on to Township Farm.

Here, if you don't like the idea of stepping stones, and these are not the most regular in the world, or if it is wet, carry on the track/road to Keld and turn left to cross the Lowther River by a bridge with no danger of getting wet.

Otherwise, carry on past some barns to turn left when you see the farmhouse and go down the track in front of the house to cross the presumed River Lowther by the lovely stepping stones. Follow the west bank of the river round to cross Keld Gill just before it joins the River Lowther, and join the minor road from Keld to Tailbert.

Follow the minor road southwest and then northwest, crossing the huge outflow pipe from Haweswater en route to thirsty Manchester mainly, and about 400 yards from Tailbert, where a small gill passes under the road, turn left on a path which can be quite boggy, which leads you obliquely down the south bounding side of lonely Swindale, past a dam, to cross the beck at a bridge. Again, there is some boggy ground to negotiate in front of the bridge.

Turn left down the road, and admire the four buttresses of Gouther Crag on the south side of the valley, a truly remote and fine place to climb.

On the Trussgap, Swindale Beck

High Loup above the head of Haweswater

At Swindale Head farm take the track up the hill on the right and follow it right again across a ford. It becomes overgrown with gorse in places but you should be able to see the definite grooved oblique course of it above to the left as it turns south of west and eventually crosses a boggy plateau, marked intermittently by posts. This is the Old Corpse Road, which took corpses by horseback from Mardale Green to burial at Shap before 1736, after which presumably the church grounds became consecrated. As it starts to descend to the right of Rowantreethwaite beck, the most fantastic view of Haweswater and High Street enfolds. You are now in the Lake District proper, and there is your lake, except that it is a reservoir.

Prior to 1929 you would have been looking down on the head of Mardale with the

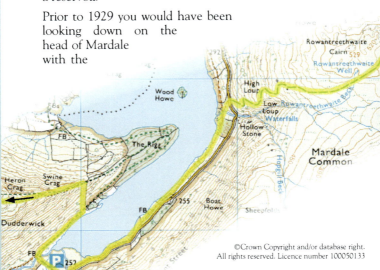

village of Mardale Green straight ahead; the church and the famous Dun Bull Inn were at each side of the tip of the afforested finger of land sticking into the Reservoir, The Rigg. Construction of the Dam started that year and flooding of the valley was in 1935, converting the two and a half mile natural lake into three and a half mile reservoir, raising the level 95 feet, and swamping Mardale Green village and Measand village further down the valley. Coffins had to removed from the churchyard to Shap, via the new road built by Manchester Corporation, not over the Old Corpse Road, and the stone from the dismantled Church was used in the Dam construction!

The path descends via some zigzags and through some ruins, High and Low Loup, which look like old mine buildings but which are largely a mystery, even Wainwright doesn't give their history. One suggestion is that they are peat huts, for storing and drying peat for use by Mardale Green village, and certainly the area you've just walked across would make good peat, at one time the major source of fuel.

Enter the lakeside road via a gate, and leave it ten yards further south by a path by the lake, which joins the road again near the car park at Mardale Head. In draught times which we are told will become more frequent, as will flooding, due to global climate changes, you may see the remains of walls, roads and bridges on your right. The last big draught was in 1984, pictures available on the Internet.

Look across the lake and spy an obvious diagonal path which you can use as a steep shortcut to get you from the lake path up to the path up Rough crag.

Carry on through the kissing gate and turn sharp right after a few yards, heading for a bridge over the Mardale beck, then swing right and go along the western lakeside path. The path you spied from the other side of the lake is quite small, and steeply ascends to join the main path up High Street just below Swine Crag.

High Street, East Ridge

You are now on one of the most direct and exhilarating ascent routes of any Lakeland peak, a not too narrow ridge with splendid views to either side, coming out virtually at the summit.

The way is obvious, except to say that between five and ten minutes from when you got onto the ridge, there is a thin path leading on, and a band of path-like rock leading diagonally backwards and upwards; take this, it's the main path. You will use your hands to aid progress in places but it isn't really scrambling.

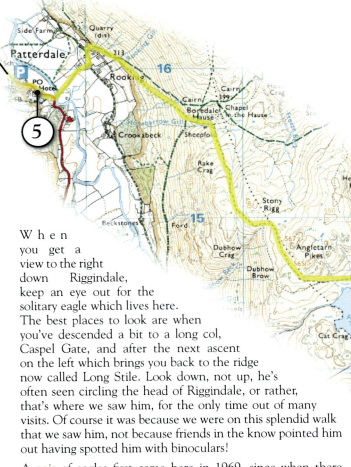

When
you get a
view to the right
down Riggindale,
keep an eye out for the
solitary eagle which lives here.
The best places to look are when
you've descended a bit to a long col,
Caspel Gate, and after the next ascent
on the left which brings you back to the ridge
now called Long Stile. Look down, not up, he's
often seen circling the head of Riggindale, or rather,
that's where we saw him, for the only time out of many
visits. Of course it was because we were on this splendid walk
that we saw him, not because friends in the know pointed him
out having spotted him with binoculars!

A pair of eagles first came here in 1969, since when there
have been various couplings and sixteen chicks produced.
Unfortunately it's not known, even by the RSPB, where they
went subsequently, if anywhere. None have fledged since
1996, and the last female left our lone eagle bloke in 2004, and
we don't know whether he's glad or sad.

After the last steep climb of Long Stile, a cairn is reached on the edge of the plateau of High Street, and if in poor visibility turn left and after a hundred yards or so another cairn appears, also near the edge, but carry on in this line and the OS trig point of the

On Rough Crag, High Street East Ridge

summit will soon appear, by a wall.

This is the highest point of the walk so far, 2718 feet or 828 metres, and gives a Lakeland panorama westwards, the sea southwards, if Morecambe Bay can be called such, and the Howgills in the south of east with the Pennines north of east.

There is line of a Roman Road running north-south over this ridge, corresponding to the Bridleway on the map, but it's a way westwards off the ridge summit,

Patterdale from Boredale Hause

so unless the wind is howling from the east (you're not doing this in winter, surely?), it's more scenic to stick to the eastern rim and descend north to a col, the Straits of Riggindale, where a large path exits right for Kidsty Pike, and which is the Coast to Coast joining us backwards!

Carry straight on, curving round the Knott and descending on a well beaten path, keeping on a northwesterly course till prison gill is crossed, when it swings westwards and passes under Satura Crag. Having read AW's Far Eastern Fells guide, you may remember that there is a fine view of Bannerdale from the top of Satura Crag, only 25 yards from the path.

Press on to curve round above Angle Tarn, and if you are lucky to see it on a sunny afternoon strip off and surprise the fishes, a wonderful place for a cool down.

Refreshed, carry on past Angletarn Pikes and descend to Boredale Hause on the map, Boardale according to AW and on my old 1974 OS map. Who changed it?

There are two paths from the Hause down to Patterdale, one from the south and one from the north, and it matters little which you take, although it is easier to turn left after crossing a stream and take the first (southern) path down.

After meeting a wall on the left the first path left takes you down very shortly to a lane where turn left, and in just over a hundred yards bear right, west, to cross Goldrill Beck and join the main road, left for the YHA or right for the hotels and a welcome drink after a long and hopefully very satisfying day.

NOTES

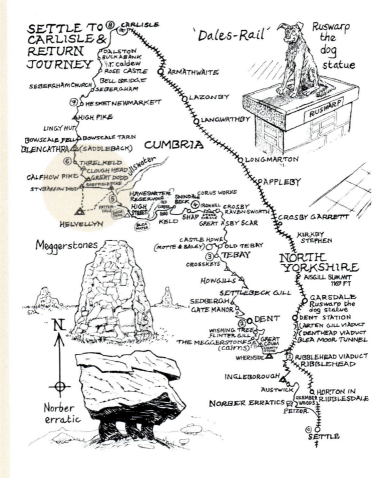

SETTLE TO CARLISLE & RETURN JOURNEY

⑧ CARLISLE
DALSTON
BUCKABANK
r. caldew
ROSE CASTLE
ARMATHWAITE
SEBERGHAM CHURCH
BELL BRIDGE
SEBERGHAM
⑦ HESKET NEW MARKET
LAZONBY
HIGH PIKE
LANGWATHBY
LINGY HUT
BOWSCALE FELL — BOWSCALE TARN
BLENCATHRA (SADDLEBACK)
CUMBRIA
LONGMARTON
⑥ THRELKELD
CLOUGH HEAD
Ullswater
CALFHOW PIKE — GREAT DODD
APPLEBY
STYBARROW DODD
SHEFFIELD PIKE
HAWESWATER RESERVOIR
SWINDALE BECK
CORUS WORKS
HIGH STREET
OLD CORPSE ROAD
④ IRON HILL
CROSBY RAVENSWORTH
CROSBY GARRETT
PATTER-DALE
SHAP STONE CIRCLE
GREAT ASBY SCAR
HELVELLYN
BLEA WATER
KELD
KIRKBY STEPHEN
CASTLE HOWE (MOTTE & BAILEY)
OLD TEBAY
Meggerstones
③ TEBAY
CROSSKEYS
NORTH YORKSHIRE
AISGILL SUMMIT 1169 FT
HOWGILLS
SETTLEBECK GILL
GARSDALE Ruswarp the dog statue
SEDBERGH
GATE MANOR
DENT STATION
ARTEN GILL VIADUCT
② DENT
DENTHEAD VIADUCT
N
WISHING TREE
FLINTER GILL
THE MEGGERSTONES (cairns)
BLEA MOOR TUNNEL
GREAT COUM
COUNTY STONE
WHERNSIDE
① RIBBLEHEAD VIADUCT
RIBBLEHEAD
INGLEBOROUGH
HORTON IN RIBBLESDALE
AUSTWICK
Norber erratic
NORBER ERRATICS
OXENBER WOODS
FEIZOR
⑨ SETTLE

'Dales-Rail'

Ruswarp the dog statue

RUSWARP

DAY 6
Patterdale to Threlkeld

**Route A: 10.7 miles (17.2 km) Ascent: 3580 ft ascent.
Via: Glenridding, Sheffield Pike, The Dodds,
Clough Head.**

**Route B: 11.1 miles (17.8 km)   Ascent: 3126 ft ascent
Route C: 12.9 miles (20.7 km)   Ascent: 4508 ft ascent**

I have given you a choice today, you consumers of landscape, because the original route, B, was planned for us over 55 year olds to be a relatively easy and direct one after a hard day yesterday, the ascent of Sticks Pass being easy, or "dull" according to AW. Subsequent reflection has led me to add two more choices. A strenuous route, C, for the younger or fitter and those who enjoy a good scramble, up Striding edge onto Helvellyn, and also the best route of all, which is the preferred route, A. This avoids the industrial scars of the Greenside Mine valley and substitutes that with excellent views of Ullswater, but is steeper and rougher, and boggier on Sheffield Pike.

All three join on Stybarrow Dodd, and the starts are the same to the south end of Rattlebeck Bridge. On the maps Route B is shown in pink when it leaves Route A, and Route C in light blue when it leaves Route B.

Route A

Head towards Glenridding by the A road, making use of the paths parallel to the road after Grisedale Beck, first to the right, then to the left.

In Glenridding turn left before the beck and follow it first on a road then on a path past the campsite, and when joined by the track coming over Rattlebeck Bridge turn right

DAY 6: PATTERDALE TO THRELKELD

Ullswater from the lower East ridge of Sheffield Pike

over the Bridge and ascend to join the main road, Greenside Road, coming up from Glenridding, at a bench and a sign with "Sticks Pass" on it. Carry on up and

round to the west and immediately after a cattle grid, take the grassy track on the right zigzagging up the fell. It appears to lead to the back of the cottages in front, but halfway there a pole with yellow path signs indicates a small but definite path to the right, which is steep, through the bracken in summer. The other path straight on curves right and ascends the dry bed of a shallow gully, and was the route in AW's books, but is direct and therefore steeper. The first path zigzags up to meet a left slanting path above Blaes Crag which leads up to a col with a wall across it. Follow the path rightwards along the wall for a short distance until another path leaves on the right to climb through bilberry and heather to the splendid viewpoint of Glenridding Dodd; Ullswater with larches in the foreground.

Retrace your steps to the col and keep on by the wall up the ridge ahead, crossing over the wall after a short climb. The interesting path zigzags its way up the lovely heathery ridge without real need to use ones hands, and occasional backwards glances reveals different views of Ullswater. There's no doubt, this is more scenic than going up through Greenside mine!

As the path levels out you can go right to the top of Heron Pike with a further view of Ullswater, or carry on across a somewhat boggy plateau-cum-broad ridge onto the summit of Sheffield Pike.

You may have noticed at various points between Glenridding Dodd and here marking posts or stones with 'M' on one side, 'H' on the other. There is one just above the first wall on the Sheffield Pike ridge, and one at the north side of the cairn on the summit. At first we thought they were welcoming "his and hers" signs just for us, but research reveals that they indicate the estates of the Marshalls of Patterdale and the Howards of Greystoke to the north. The wild East!

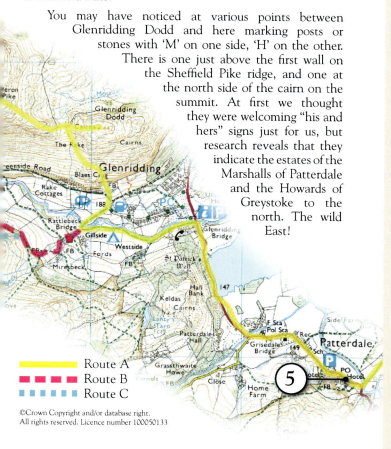

Route A
Route B
Route C

From Glenridding Dodd West to Raise (centre right), with, from the left, Birkhouse Moor, Catstye Cam and Helvellyn Lower Man

Estate marker Stones, near summit of Sheffield Pike

Route A
Route B
Route C

The graceful pyramid of Catstycam is prominent in front of Helvellyn off to your left, if you can see it. We couldn't.

A slightly boggy descent to the col of Nick Head is followed by an ascent up a path on the grassy ridge leading northwest and up to White Stones. You cannot really escape the industrial blight by taking this route, with spoil evident and a large quarry so prominent from Route B in "death valley" below, passed by very closely on the left, be careful!

If you are in mist, there are three cairns on White Stones, or perhaps more correctly, "White Stones top of Greenside," to guide you: the summit is rather low and rounded and you might think you are back on the Howgills.

The large disused quarry and spoil heaps around Sticks Gill, from the path up to White Stones of Greenside

Carry on due west a down grassy slope to a broad col, and then up the grass slope, in some previous guides stated to be pathless but certainly there is a path to start with, up Stybarrow Dodd, at first westerly and then northwesterly. As you come to the top of the dome, the true summit is a cairn with an upright spike of slate. North-east of here about a hundred yards away is a broken wall to help in poor visibility. This is above of a little crag, Deepdale Crag, which in turn is above a gill, which is a tributary of, or maybe even the source of Aira Beck, which gives rise to the well known beauty spot of Aira Force just before entering Ullswater.

This summit, identified by AW as the true summit, may surprise you, as it is the highest point of your walk so far at 2768 feet (843 metres), being 50 feet or 15 metres higher than High Street.

When AW was writing his guides in the '50s, he corrected the Ordnance Survey over the height of this fell, the summit of which was thought to be at the southwestern end of

Summit cairn on Stybarrow Dodd. Skiddaw and Blencathra in the distance

the ridge, at 2756 feet, and he estimated the now accepted summit to be 2770 feet, about 300 yards northeast. Two feet out, not bad!

The grassy dome, it has to be said, is entirely dull, but the panorama magnificent. If you are meeting friends here from route B they

The Dodds

should be here by now, but in view of the above, make sure you are both meeting on the same summit! They will have dryer feet. You'll have to wait for any friends scrambling up route C, they may be a while and if they've any decency will look very tired.

When any planned reunion has been successful, continue "doing the Dodds", all of which are Wainwrights.

A tootle down to the main path again and on to Watson's Dodd is followed by reascent to Great Dodd, which is now our new highest point of the walk, 2813 feet (the OS have upgraded the height since

Wainwright's 1955 guide gave it 2807 feet), or 857 metres. You can tell there's not much interest on the ground as I am having to dwell on heights, but the views remain magnificent, particularly westwards. Carrying Wainwright's Eastern Fells book will enable you to identify the hills on view.

Regain the main path to the west and go down the slope to the Tor of Calfhow Pike, then swing northwards on the path to Clough Head, first descending and then ascending. Because there are steep crags to the north and west of Clough Head, Wainwright advises to avoid it in bad

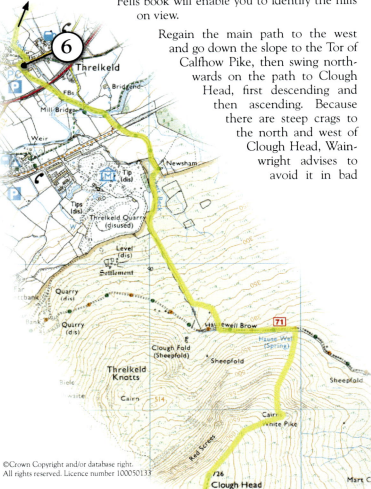

weather, but the top is easily identifiable with an OS column and cairn, and from here the descent is safe if you take a bearing for White Pike, and a path appears on the way to it, skirting it to the left and continuing safely on a thin grassy path north of northeast to reach the old coach

Threlkeld and Blencathra from Clough Head

road from Dockray to St John's in the Vale at a stile.

Turn left here on the old coach road, fenced on its southside only. Eventually you are heading north and down towards Threlkeld Quarry alongside the obvious fence, the easiest and driest way being to skirt this side of what looks like an old railway carriage, missing the marshy ground. This is open access land without a definite path. Cross Birkett Beck and go through a gate giving access to a track by Newsham, which leads down to the River Glenderamackin and across it via a bridge.

The Quarry you passed on your left side is for granite, and a museum of mining and quarrying exists in the site, with an "underground experience"!

The pleasantest way into the delightful village of Threlkeld –the thralls' spring (norse)- is to follow the Glenderamackin westwards on a path which turns north after the Kilnhow beck, to cross the A66, easily the most dangerous part of the whole trip. A field path leads into the village by the church. Watch out for red squirrels here.

The church of St Mary's is not the most charming in the world, having been built in 1776 on the site of a previous one, from which the existing 600 year old bells were transferred.

Route B

Follow Route A to where the track coming over Rattlebeck Bridge joins your path, then turn left up the hill, following Mires beck, deviating left from it then coming back to it to pass through a gate onto open access land. Turn immediately right and follow the almost level path above Glenridding Beck to the footbridge over it in just under a mile.

The first shoulder you go round after joining the level path is a better, more rough way up Helvellyn, Route C, but you have chosen the more sedate option, so carry onwards.

Over the footbridge turn right downstream for a short distance then up to join the main track up from Glenridding, Greenside Road. Turn left onto this track, signposted "Brown Cove, Whiteside Bank, Sticks Pass" and pass through what remains of the Greenside Mine smelting works. After a short distance up turn right on a path marked "Sticks Pass", which zig-zags up the hillside through gorse and then traverses a weird looking valley where the ravages of past lead mining are very evident. This may not be the most beautiful valley in the Lakes but it is not dull; atmospheric is the word. The bed of a reservoir and various water channels are evident, spoil heaps, and quarries, particularly impressive of which in mist is the yawning chasm seen north on the eastern end of Greenside. It may have been mostly green once.

Greenside Mine

This is of some interest, not just to offset this route being supposedly dull. AW did not have access to the Internet.

Lead had been mined here since the 17th Century, but the mine itself was set up in 1818 and ceased as a company in the late 1950s, when the UK Atomic Energy Research Establishment took it over and two atomic explosions were conducted underground, named Operation Orpheus, to see if a seismic signal could be detected from such activity. As a result, a test ban treaty between the West and The USSR was shelved as it proved that such a ban could not be policed by the other side! Final closure was in 1961.

The ore extracted from the rock was called Galena, which is lead sulphide, from which 80% by weight is lead, and 12% silver, the latter sold on to the treasury. Lead was used for pipes, roofing, and bullets, many of which were shot in the American Civil War. Later uses were in paint, in glass making, pottery glazing and in enamel.

The mine was the first to use (hydro) electric energy, for powering the winding gear used in smelting, from the end of the 19th Century until 1936, when the National Grid came in, the water coming from Red Tarn, and Keppel Cove Tarn. You can see a complex of water leats all over the valleys. Keppel Cove Tarn burst its banks following a cloudburst in 1927 destroying the Bridge near Ullswater, though no-one was killed, and the Dam itself was breached four years later so the message from the nature Gods was finally heeded and the damage not repaired.

The efficient use of hydroelectric energy, was the main reason that the mine survived the downturn in lead prices in the late 19th Century, when others e.g. in Swaledale, closed down.

After closure most of the buildings were taken down, except those downstream from the bridge, which are now used as hostels (the YHA and outdoor activity groups).

The path turns west after crossing "death valley", and gradually climbs away from it on the flank of Greenside, following Sticks Gill on the left increasingly steeply but easily up to Sticks Pass, which at 2420 feet is the highest pass in Lakeland, Wainwright tells us, crossed by a path in common use. His Eastern Fells Guide was finished in December 1954, when interestingly the Ski tow which is now clearly visible on the north side of Raise was there, but not the ski hut.

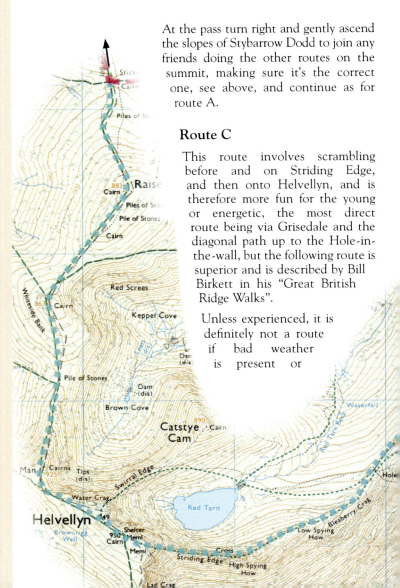

At the pass turn right and gently ascend the slopes of Stybarrow Dodd to join any friends doing the other routes on the summit, making sure it's the correct one, see above, and continue as for route A.

Route C

This route involves scrambling before and on Striding Edge, and then onto Helvellyn, and is therefore more fun for the young or energetic, the most direct route being via Grisedale and the diagonal path up to the Hole-in-the-wall, but the following route is superior and is described by Bill Birkett in his "Great British Ridge Walks".

Unless experienced, it is definitely not a route if bad weather is present or forecast.

Follow route B until you meet the rocky shoulder on your left on the almost level path above Glenridding Beck, and ascend it avoiding the rocky bluffs or scrambling as it suits you, to reach The Nab and then Birkhouse Moor cairn. Follow the ridge on an increasingly wide path to negotiate Striding Edge with as much scrambling, again, as you desire, but some will be required at the end, before the steep final pull up scree to the summit ridge.

The last time I came up here, alone in December, my map was blown out of my cagoule pocket without me realising it, and there was no visibility and a howling gale. Thankfully the way onto Swirral Edge is well marked and visibility came half-way down Catstycam. Do you know, I saw no-one from the path above Glenridding Beck till I reached it again.

▬▬▬▬	Route A
▬ ▬ ▬ ▬	Route B
▪ ▪ ▪ ▪ ▪ ▪	Route C

Striding Edge approaching Helvellyn

Hopefully you can see the way, past the exit to Swirral Edge, but around 600 yards from the summit you have to keep awake and fork north off the main path, which goes to Thirlspot, and ascend slightly to Lower Man, followed by a descent of a rocky ridge to a col and an ascent of the grassy ridge to White Side. The signs lower down and the Ordnance survey now call this summit Whiteside Bank. At the cairned summit you must again make a conscious effort, even in good weather, to turn right, northeast, or you may end up descending another path to Thirlspot northwest.

The wide highway descends to a col where keep straight on as another huge highway forks right to curve round Raise and descend to Glenridding. The straight on highway ascends to Raise, another dome but with many rough pumice like rocks at the northern end unlike any other summit in the Helvellyn/Dodds ridge, and a further down leads you to Sticks pass and Route B, then route A on Stybarrow Dodd which see and follow home.

To be consistent with the theme of Route A above, I must add that on Route C, Helvellyn would be the highest point of the whole trip at 3118 feet (950m), and both of the Wainwrights White Side (2832/863) and Raise (2889/883) are mightier in height than the Dodds north of Sticks Pass.

NOTES

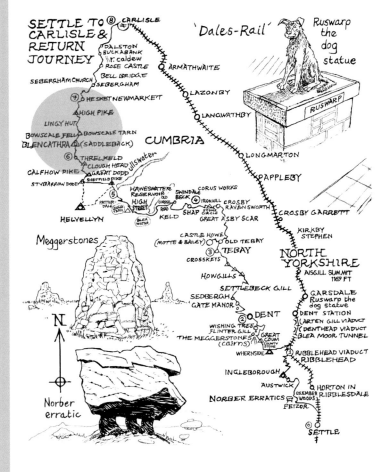

SETTLE TO CARLISLE & RETURN JOURNEY

'Dales-Rail'

Ruswarp the dog statue

RUSWARP

⑧ CARLISLE

DALSTON
BUCKABANK
r. caldew
ROSE CASTLE
BELL BRIDGE
SEBERGHAM
SEBERGHAM CHURCH
⑦ HESKET NEWMARKETT
HIGH PIKE
LINGY HUT
BOWSCALE FELL BOWSCALE TARN
BLENCATHRA (SADDLEBACK)
⑥ THRELKELD
CLOUGH HEAD
GREAT DODD
CALFHOW PIKE
STYBARROW DODD
⑤ HIGH STREET
PATTER-DALE
HELVELLYN
SHEFFIELD PIKE
GLEN COYNE FARM
BLEA WATER
HAWESWATER RESERVOIR
SWINDALE BECK
④ IRONHILL
CORPSE ROAD
SHAP STONE CIRCLE
KELD
GREAT ASBY SCAR
CORUS WORKS
CROSBY RAVENSWORTH
CASTLE HOWE (MOTTE & BAILEY)
③ OLD TEBAY
TEBAY
CROSSKEYS
HOWGILLS
SETTLEBECK GILL
SEDBERGH
GATE MANOR
② DENT
WISHING TREE
FLINTER GILL
THE MEGGERSTONES (cairns)
GREAT COUM
COUNTY STONE
WHERNSIDE
INGLEBOROUGH
AUSTWICK
NORBER ERRATICS
OXEMBER WOODS
FEIZOR
⑥ SETTLE

ARMATHWAITE
LAZONBY
LANGWATHBY
LONGMARTON
APPLEBY
CROSBY GARRETT
KIRKBY STEPHEN
NORTH YORKSHIRE
AISGILL SUMMIT 1169 FT
GARSDALE Ruswarp the dog statue
DENT STATION
ARTEN GILL VIADUCT
DENTHEAD VIADUCT
BLEA MOOR TUNNEL
RIBBLEHEAD VIADUCT
RIBBLEHEAD
HORTON IN RIBBLESDALE

CUMBRIA

Ullswater

Meggerstones

N

Norber erratic

DAY 7
Threlkeld to
Hesket Newmarket

Distance: 11.9 miles (19.1 km) Ascent: 4167 feet
Via: Blencathra, (Halls Fell), Bowscale Fell
and Tarn, High Pike.

The greatest days ascent of the walk today, (excepting the Helvellyn alternative yesterday), and not twelve miles.

It's a sunny day and you look out of your window and see the magnificent frontage of Blencathra. Which way up? The three routes facing you from your accommodation are steep, the nearest one and the furthest west is Gategill Fell, which is the steepest in the lower section

Blencathra with Hall's Fell (right of centre)

and hard to find a path through heather from below, but a delight once Knott Halloo is reached; the furthest away east is Doddick Fell, the easiest of all, but the best in most people's books is the middle one, Hall's Fell, which does have some mild scrambling in places and is a bit airy for some, including Margaret, who coped with it well this time. Vies with the East ridge of High Street (and Striding Edge for Route B-ers) for the finest way up a hill on this walk, but is more exciting. So this is the described way.

Get onto the path to Gategill either from the main road in Threlkeld just west of Kilnhow Beck, or from just alongside the "No Through Road" to Blencathra Centre, which is the old Sanatorium in Wainwrights' guide, depending on your place of stay.

Cross Kilnhow Beck and follow the path across fields to Gategill, where turn left and up to cross the Gate Gill when the open fell is reached. The path goes diagonally up the Fell with wonderful views all the way, although you may prefer to look where you're going when the arête proper is reached, indeed Margaret looked at it for quite some time! It leads you absolutely straight up to the summit cairn. Bingo.

After the customary loll about, pictures etc of the extensive panorama, and waiting for members of your group afflicted by paralysis of high places (perhaps you should have been helping them?), make off towards the cairn of Atkinson Pike, either directly via the small tarn, which is on the saddle of the alternative name so loathed by Wainwright, Saddleback, very obvious when viewed from the east, or if you haven't seen the famous Sharp Edge, keep to the path round the edge which gives a fine view of the same and Scales Tarn.

Now Sharp Edge does involve definite scrambling, and is a fine

route, until the arête has finished and then a steep slope with some loose rock and a nasty gully comes along. Definitely a route for a dry day. Margaret was offered this route some years ago but demured half way along, quite wisely as it turned out, a massive thunderstorm making progress very

On Hall's Fells narrow edge

worrying, but also proving that Doddick Fell is a safe way down (and up) even when running with water and the drops are rebounding 18 inches in the air!

Ten yards after the summit cairn of Atkinson Pike, another cairn marks the start of the path descending Blue Screes to the left, not at all difficult, but you may wish to survey the skyline northwards if you haven't already from Hallsfell top. High Pike, your last peak of the day and, alas, of this trip is more or less due north, and Carlisle visible to its right. The end (sob!).

At the bottom of Blue Screes the path curves round north and soon you will see, at this time of day, the shadowy and sinister looking Sharp Edge final slope from the other side. Continue to the Glenderamackin Col and across it, taking the left branch of the path, the right one going up to Bannerdale Crags and down to Mungrisdale.

Press on towards Bowscale Fell, another "Wainwright" for you, picking your way round the worst of the boggy bits on the long col between Bannerdale Crags and Bowscale Fell. Carry on the same line on the other side of the summit but when

84

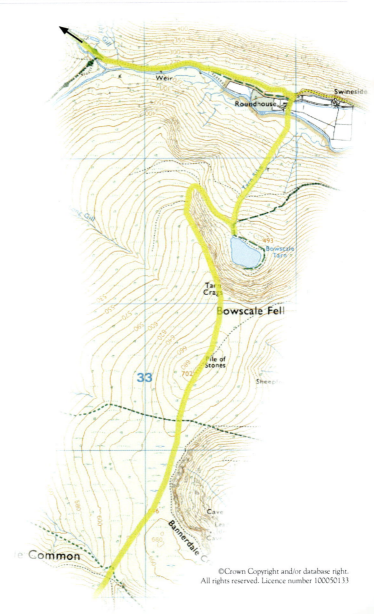

Weir

Swineside

Roundhouse

493
Bowscale
Tarn

Tarn
Crag

Bowscale Fell

33

Pile of
Stones

702

Sheep

Cave

Bannerdale

Common

you see a thin path going off on the left, the main path heading for the next summit, " Pile of Stones" on the map, on the ridge down to Mungrisdale, go down this left branch, heading for the edge, with Carrock Fell obvious in the distance. When you meet the edge, go down the rim of Bowscale Tarn Crags on an intermittent path, hopefully not in low cloud or mist, with a view of the picturesque tarn eventually. About halfway down there is a path on the right which initially has a bit of scree in it and may look unfriendly in the wet, but after the first two hundred yards or so a zigzag eases the angle and takes you down to the tarn. In fact this path is a continuation of the track coming up gently from Bowscale hamlet. If this looks too steep for you, a much gentler grassy path curves round the northern end of these crags to run down to join a grassy path descending on the west side of Tarn Sike, and before that, two grassy sheep paths.

The Tarn is very secretive and atmospheric, with an impressive moraine, much more obviously a glacial structure than, say, Stickle Tarn. Victorian Gentlefolk included the Tarn in their "Grand Tour of the Lakes", but AW found the main path to be in disrepair. Not so now, a main highway up from Bowscale hamlet.

The grassy path on the west side of Tarn Sike leads down to a footbridge at Roundhouse, open to the public, which was obviously not there in AW's time.

The view of Mosedale coming down from the Tarn is splendid, the rough boulder strewn slopes of Carrock Fell opposite dotted with

Bowscale Tarn. The two descent paths for the walk on the facing flank are obliterated by snow

gorse in the spring are offset by the green pastures downstream of Roundhouse.

Up at the road from Mosedale, turn left and trudge up to the Cumbria Way, which is a right fork up a mine track just before the road crosses the Grainsgill Beck and ends. Should you imagine that the path marked on the map from the Roundhouse track running parallel to the road for 500 yards or so might be a good idea for the feet, don't; it descends into bog every ten yards or so and doesn't really exist.

The Carrock mine site is about 400 yards up the partially tarmaced track, where it turns "green". The mine was a source of Wolfram, which crossword aficionados will recognise as Tungsten, although strictly speaking it is a source of Tungsten, and as this was used in armaments, the mine was active during both world wars.

The official Cumbria way becomes a bit rutted further on, so our route deviates right on a more direct route for the Lingy Hut, a wooden unlocked bothy. This direct path is not marked accurately on the Explorer Map, so pay attention!

The Lingy Hut

After the mine site and exactly on crossing Brandy Gill the green track slopes upwards, and where it does a zig-zag, leave it where a low ruined wall is on the right. Head obliquely upwards towards a distinct but low mound, over which the path goes and becomes more obvious and then levels off and crosses the Arm o' Grain stream. On the far side the clear path climbs roughly alongside the stream and after crossing a small side stream and steepening, turns left away from the Arm o' Grain. Continuing fairly steeply it divides, the left hand branch being the main one although boggier. This eases off exactly at a low isolated boulder, when the Lingy Hut magically comes into view a few hundred yards away.

At the Hut turn right on the broad track, which used to be for miners, to rise over the small mound of Hare Stones. As the next dip is approached, take a small but definite path leftwards before the lowest point, which heads for your last hill or Fell of the walk, the mighty High Pike, a non-pike looking grassy dome. If you can see it. If you miss the smaller path in mist a larger one veers left from the main miners' track in the dip, to gently ascend to a summit with a trig point, memorial bench and large cairn which the south wind appears to have blown a tail off to join up with the trig point. The northerly view is extensive, the north Cumbrian plain with Wigton and

Summit of High Pike

Carlisle evident and beyond the Solway Firth and Scottish hills, with the Pennines to the east. Behind you is mostly Blencathra and Skiddaw. Say goodbye and descend off the Lakeland fells to Hesket Newmarket and the famous micro-brewery pub.

The best way is not as shown on the Explorer map, but from the ruined Shepherds hut a hundred yards north of the summit, bear slightly west of north when a good path is met which descends to meet the contouring path marked on the map. Turn right on this to meet the first of the many mining remains, Potts Gill. Bear left at a junction to run down the east side of Potts Gill, continuing as the map suggests, through a gate and down to Nether Row.

The mines around here and the ore taken from them gave rise to the well-known expression "Caldbeck hills are worth all England else", it's not a scenic compari- son. Barytes was the last mineral mined, still pro- duced when AW wrote

Descending High Pike, Caldbeck North Cumbrian plain ahead

his Northern Fells Guide, and only ceased in 1966. Barytes is barium sulphate, an inert non toxic compound, now used mainly in fluids

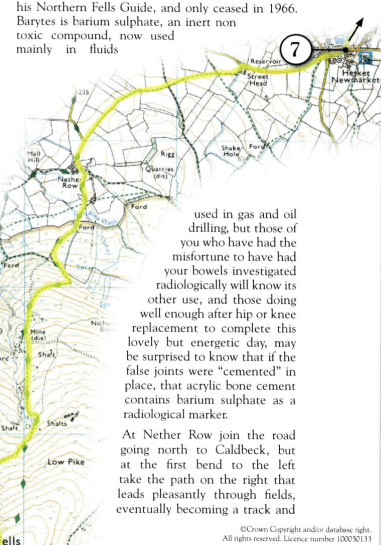

used in gas and oil drilling, but those of you who have had the misfortune to have had your bowels investigated radiologically will know its other use, and those doing well enough after hip or knee replacement to complete this lovely but energetic day, may be surprised to know that if the false joints were "cemented" in place, that acrylic bone cement contains barium sulphate as a radiological marker.

At Nether Row join the road going north to Caldbeck, but at the first bend to the left take the path on the right that leads pleasantly through fields, eventually becoming a track and

Hesket Newmarket

joining another road at Street Head.

Turn right and tootle down to Hesket, straight into The Old Crown for a welcome pint of one of their beers on show. The micro-brewery started in 1988 when Jim and Liz Fearnley bought the pub, with Jim the brewer. When he retired in 1999 the locals understandably did not want the brewery to be swallowed by a big brewery so 58 of them formed a cooperative and bought it, and when the pub was up for sale again in 2002, to protect the link between the brewery and the pub, another local cooperative of 125 locals this time bought the pub, believed to be the first such pub in Britain. It is a splendid friendly local, and as it is justifiably famous does get busy at weekends. We arrived on a Wednesday and it was not overrun, just what a pub should be.

NOTES

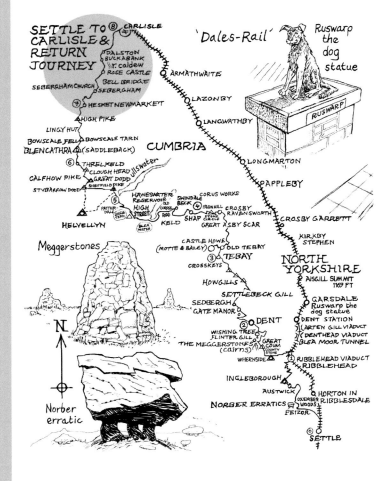

SETTLE TO CARLISLE & RETURN JOURNEY

'Dales-Rail'

Ruswarp the dog statue

CARLISLE ⑧

DALSTON
BUCKABANK
r. caldew
ROSE CASTLE
BELL BRIDGE
SEBERGHAM
SEBERGHAM CHURCH

ARMATHWAITE

HESKET NEWMARKET ⑦

LAZONBY

HIGH PIKE

LINGY HUT

LANGWATHBY

BOWSCALE FELL   BOWSCALE TARN
BLENCATHRA (SADDLEBACK)

CUMBRIA

THRELKELD ⑥
CLOUGH HEAD
GREAT DODD
Ullswater

LONGMARTON

CALFHOW PIKE
SHEFFIELD PIKE
STYBARROW DODD

APPLEBY

HAWESWATER
RESERVOIR
SHINDALE
BECK
OLD CORPSE
ROAD
CORUS WORKS
IRONHILL
STONE
CIRCLE
CROSBY
RAVENSWORTH

⑤
HIGH STREET
PATTER-DALE
SHAP

KELD

GREAT ASBY SCAR

CROSBY GARRETT

HELVELLYN
BLEA
WATER

Meggerstones

N

Norber
erratic

KIRKBY
STEPHEN

CASTLE HOWE
(MOTTE & BAILEY)   OLD TEBAY
③ TEBAY
CROSSKEYS

NORTH
YORKSHIRE

AISGILL SUMMIT
1169 FT

HOWGILLS

GARSDALE
Ruswarp the
dog statue
DENT STATION
ARTEN GILL VIADUCT
DENTHEAD VIADUCT
BLEA MOOR TUNNEL

SETTLEBECK GILL

SEDBERGH
GATE MANOR   ② DENT

WISHING TREE
FLINTER GILL
THE MEGGERSTONES
(cairns)
GREAT
COUM
COUNTY
STONE

WHERNSIDE

RIBBLEHEAD VIADUCT ①
RIBBLEHEAD

INGLEBOROUGH

AUSTWICK
NORBER ERRATICS
OXENBER
WOODS
FEIZOR

HORTON IN
RIBBLESDALE

SETTLE ⓪

93

DAY 8
Hesket Newmarket
to Carlisle

Distance: 14.4 miles (23.1 km) Ascent: 703 feet
Via the Cumbria Way, following the River Caldew.

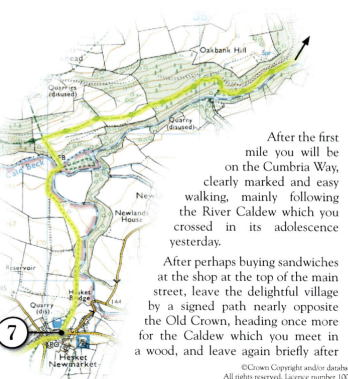

After the first mile you will be on the Cumbria Way, clearly marked and easy walking, mainly following the River Caldew which you crossed in its adolescence yesterday.

After perhaps buying sandwiches at the shop at the top of the main street, leave the delightful village by a signed path nearly opposite the Old Crown, heading once more for the Caldew which you meet in a wood, and leave again briefly after

High Pike and the Northern Fells from above the Caldew

the wood to cross a field, where the path passes between the Caldew and the Cald Beck. Curiously the Cald Beck looks the bigger of the two here, although its catchment is clearly less. Either last night's splendid beer has odd powers or water has been taken from the Caldew.

Cross the Cald Beck on a footbridge and follow the path up a gorse filled slope to a stile, after which turn right, and you are now on the Cumbria Way.

If you haven't got a copy of the "Cumbria Way", I will write some briefer notes for you.

Continue across the open land with scattered gorse for about 750 yards and enter woodland, where a path leads onto a forest track, which you have to turn right off at a gate across the track, heading down the slope to the Caldew. Follow the river to exit the trees by a gate, then veering away from the river along the wood side. This becomes a track and joins the Caldew again just before you come out onto the B road from Penrith to Wigton.

Cross the bridge and up the hill, turning left on a path after a house. This climbs the hill obliquely before turning sharp right and going through a bridlegate and onto a metalled road which leads to Sedbergham Church, a visit to which will give you a pleasant interlude. A hermit called William Wastell cleared part of what was then Inglewood Forest here in 1188, "disgusted by the lawlessness of the times", nothing changed then, and built a cell and a chapel. The chapel was later replaced by the church, although when, no-one knows.

Straight ahead from the church gate another gate leads you northwards on a track, veering right to avoid Sedbergham Hall, and on to join a minor road and turn left over the single arch of Bell Bridge. Immediately over it turn right down stone steps to continue by the Caldew. If the cows permit, this spot is a good place for a mid morning "coffee" break.

For just over the next two miles you are on the path by the Caldew and can't go wrong. To- wards the end of this stretch at

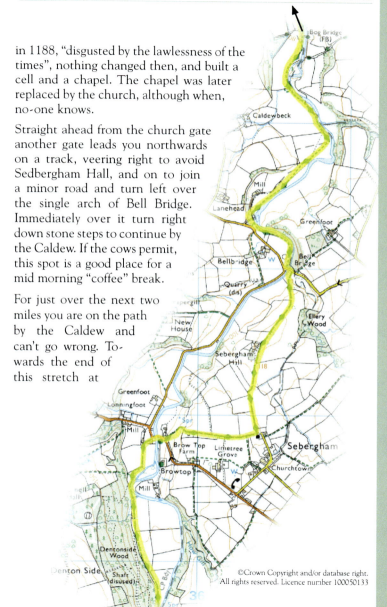

96

Rose Bridge you will see on the left Rose Castle, for 700 years the official home of the Bishops of Carlisle. The Pele tower dates from 1340, built to protect against marauding Scots returning the amorous advances of Edward I towards their country, but the house was destroyed by Parliamentarians in the Civil War and was restored much later.

A path leads left from the B road crossing Rose Bridge to the Castle grounds, which you may view if you wish but only from the path as they are private, and therefore unless you are going to risk the naughtiness of walking up the Lime House School drive after passing round the Castle grounds and going 500 yards north on the B road, it's a there and back walk.

Steps lead up to the B road which you cross to descend to the bank again and press on, leaving the Caldew as it curves back to the right after going left, a path crossing the grass towards the left edge of the wood, Willowclose Wood, which looms ahead, and pass through a kissing-gate. You are now in park-

Meadow Cranesbill. Throughout in Summer.

land, which you cross to enter the grounds of Lime House, a school, turning left on a track, across the drive and through a gate onto more parkland. Head across this to a gate and a track leading round Holmhill farm to the left, and turn right on the road to Hawksdale Hall, where a gate on the right leads onto a track, which heads north for 800 yards or so and turns sharp left and onto the B5299. This marks the end of the rural walk, from now on its suburbia, railways, mills, schools and Carlisle, different from the hills but not as boring as it may sound. Turn right on the B road to Bridge End and over the bridge. Here the official, written Cumbria Way carries on the Road, but on the Explorer map is shown as going right, and so we will do this to avoid the road. Immediately after the bridge turn right along a path signposted Raughton Road, between the Caldew and a yard of some houses with a high metal fence, the purpose of which may become evident in which case you will be thankful for it. At the end of this fence there are posts with yellow path signs pointing everywhere; just turn left and go through the white gates. You are still separated from the trained killers. A short distance on another white gate makes you feel even safer, then quickly right over a stile marked with a yellow pole marker, and along

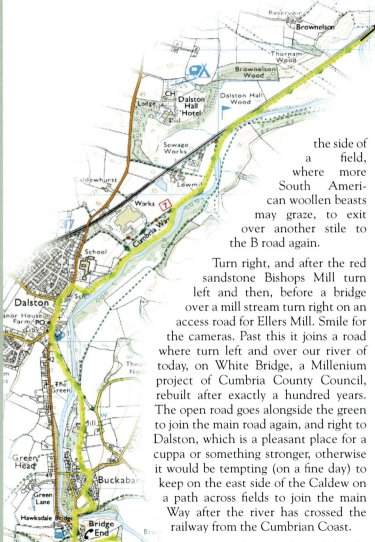

the side of a field, where more South American woollen beasts may graze, to exit over another stile to the B road again.

Turn right, and after the red sandstone Bishops Mill turn left and then, before a bridge over a mill stream turn right on an access road for Ellers Mill. Smile for the cameras. Past this it joins a road where turn left and over our river of today, on White Bridge, a Millenium project of Cumbria County Council, rebuilt after exactly a hundred years. The open road goes alongside the green to join the main road again, and right to Dalston, which is a pleasant place for a cuppa or something stronger, otherwise it would be tempting (on a fine day) to keep on the east side of the Caldew on a path across fields to join the main Way after the river has crossed the railway from the Cumbrian Coast.

You may also be tempted, in Dalston, to head for the station and take the train into Carlisle, but that would not be finishing the walk, which is Settle to Carlisle and then back by the railway, so have your drink and press on, it's only 4.8 miles to the magical station finish in Carlisle!

Carry on past the square in Dalston on the main road and turn right on a path after a primary school. This is now a hard surfaced cycle way, the Caldew Cycleway, but be not downhearted, contrary to what you may read elsewhere, there are softer options for the feet, the first coming after you have passed the Caldew School sports fields, where the marked way turns left from the river and then right to pass the Nestle factory, but a soft, permissive path carries straight on by the river here to rejoin past the factory.

The way continues to pass alongside the Cumbrian Coast Railway line for around a mile, when it passes under the line through a "low bridge" to join a metalled road leading to a factory entrance. A path continues between the factory and the Caldew, and at the end another soft path option exists by the river for about a 1000 yards, while the cycleway rises up a bank

The cycleway rejoins us at a gate and a road now passes a disused mill and an urban pub, past sports fields and then it appears to stop where Metcalfe Street ends on the left. Do not be tempted to press on by a sort of path by the river, hoping it will lead somewhere eventually because people have travelled this way

Not far to go!

100

before. They all have double footprints, there and back, and some of them were ours.

As Metcalfe Street joins Denton Street turn right, over the Caldew saying a fond farewell, on over the Victoria Viaduct, right at English Street and between the two towers of the Citadel, built in the 19C to replace the original southern entrance to the City. This seems like a good official end to the walk, and the station is just a right turn away. That's it! Well done and I hope you enjoyed it!

I also hope you are not met by a whole mounted police force as we were; guiltily wondering what we had done, I suddenly realised it was footballs' play-off time, and the football team of my adolescence, Leeds United, were playing Carlisle. In the old third division, how are the mighty indeed, and they didn't get promoted then either!

Carlisle

The "castle (caer) of Luel", The Border City: the administrative centre of Cumbria, and the main shopping, commercial and industrial centre for north Cumbria and a large part of southern Scotland.

One of the two towers of Carlisle's Citadel, and the finish of the walk.

The Romans called their settlement between the Eden, The Caldew and the Petteril, Luguvallium. It was here to service Hadrian's Wall, the fortified camp on the wall being just over the Eden northwards, where Stanwix is now.

The town was destroyed by the Vikings in 875, and reclaimed by the Norman King William Rufus in 1092, who started building the castle and walls around the town, some of which can be seen today. The castle was finished by King David 1 of Scotland, illustrating nicely the see-saw fate of this border town. It is now the home of the Border Regiment, the museum giving a good history of the area and regiment. If your time is limited, I would recommend this as your first visit.

The Cathedral is the other monument worth a visit, built of red sandstone, and originally built in 1122 as a priory by Henry the 1st. A greater part of the nave was destroyed by a Scots army in the 17th Century. The Decorated-style east window is made mainly from mediaeval stained glass and is the largest East window of any European Cathedral, and the most complex Flowing Decorated Gothic Style window in England.

In the late 18th Century the town became a densely populated cotton mill town, which led to it becoming a

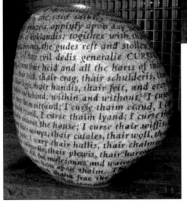

The "Cursing Stone"

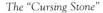

railway town also. The Station is an important part of the city: in the 19th Century it had seven different companies all with separate goods yards using it. The building, by Sir William Tite, was in a Tudor Gothic style to harmonise with the Citadel, the twin Towers and original southern entrance to the city, where the walk finished.

Two other facts about Carlisle are worth mentioning: the first is that from 1916 to 1919 you couldn't buy a round in a Carlisle pub, (or the surrounding district)! This is because of a government initiative called the State Management Scheme, basically the state took over the management of the pubs and breweries, to introduce an ethos of disinterested management and discourage drinking and drunkenness, which in 1916 was affecting the workforce in the nearby Gretna munitions factory somewhat negatively. The Cromwellian sounding New Model Inn Style was developed here during this initiative, and unfortunately spread elsewhere like a rash. That nice Mr Heath abolished this nonsense in 1973. Carlisle was not alone, two other areas were picked on.

The second fact of interest is the Curse of Carlisle, a 16C formal curse by Archbishop Dunbar of Glasgow, really against the border Reivers, who stole cattle and generally were not very nice neighbours. A large granite rock with the thousand plus words of the curse engraved thereon was commissioned by the local council, as a Millenium project. It was installed in an underpass between the Castle and Tullie house Museum, (incidentally worth visiting), but not before objections by Christian campaigners.

Subsequently an unholy coalition between a Liberal Democrat Councillor and the Christian campaigners (possibly a blueprint for our current government in 2010?) were blaming the foot and mouth outbreak of 2001, which originated near here, and the severe floods of January 2005, and probably their Aunty Mabel's prolapse on the Curse. A self-titled "God of all witches" joined in the controversy, pompously declaring that moving the "stone" would give it more power, but rather more sensibly pointing out that a curse can only work if people believe in it. The latter advice was taken, maybe, because the stone still stands!

If you want to read the curse in the underpass, and worry that reading it while completing a circle constitutes an occult ritual, I can categorically reassure you that if you went three times round the roots of the wishing tree in Flinter Gill above Dent, (clockwise of course) or intend to at any time in the future, you are not!

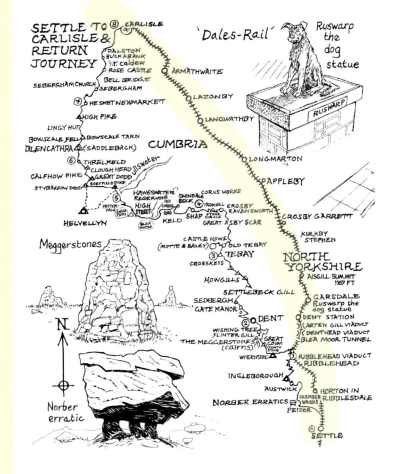

SETTLE TO CARLISLE & RETURN JOURNEY

⑧ CARLISLE
DALSTON
BUCKABANK
r. caldew
ROSE CASTLE
BELL BRIDGE
SEBERGHAM CHURCH
SEBERGHAM
ARMATHWAITE
'Dales-Rail'

⑦ HESKET NEWMARKET
HIGH PIKE
LINGY HUT
BOWSCALE FELL BOWSCALE TARN
BLENCATHRA △ (SADDLEBACK)
CUMBRIA
LAZONBY
LANGWATHBY

⑥ THRELKELD
CLOUGH HEAD
GREAT DODD
CALFHOW PIKE
STYBARROW DODD
SHEFFIELD PIKE
Ullswater
LONGMARTON
APPLEBY

HAWESWATER RESERVOIR
SHINDALE BECK
CORUS WORKS
⑤ HIGH STREET
PATTER DALE
OLD CORPSE ROAD
④ IRONHILL
STONE CIRCLE
CROSBY RAVENSWORTH
CROSBY GARRETT
HELVELLYN
BLEA WATER
KELD
SHAP
GREAT ASBY SCAR

Meggerstones
CASTLE HOWE (MOTTE & BAILEY) OLD TEBAY
③ TEBAY
CROSSKEYS
KIRKBY STEPHEN
NORTH YORKSHIRE
AISGILL SUMMIT 1169 FT

HOWGILLS
SETTLEBECK GILL
SEDBERGH
GATE MANOR
② DENT
GARSDALE Ruswarp the dog statue
DENT STATION
ARTEN GILL VIADUCT
DENTHEAD VIADUCT
BLEA MOOR TUNNEL

N

WISHING TREE
FLINTER GILL
THE MEGGERSTONES (cairns)
GREAT COUM
COUNTY STONE
WHERNSIDE
① RIBBLEHEAD VIADUCT
RIBBLEHEAD

Norber erratic

INGLEBOROUGH
AUSTWICK
NORBER ERRATICS OXEMBER WOODS
FEIZOR
HORTON IN RIBBLESDALE

⑩ SETTLE

Ruswarp the dog statue
RUSWARP

⑩ 105

THE SETTLE TO CARLISLE RAILWAY

It must be said straight off that this is not exactly the Jungfrau railway. It goes through some hills but does not provide a north-face mountain view! Nevertheless it is the most scenic railway in England, 72 miles long and with 14 tunnels and 17 major viaducts,

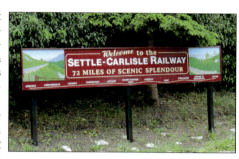

Sign at Settle Station

the finest and most photographed you walked by at Ribblehead. Oh, and the Jungfrau line was 30 years later.

HISTORY

It's history is interesting: the company which built it, the Midland Railway company, (MR), didn't actually want to build it in 1869, when work started, being forced to when Parliament, after an eight day session in April of that year, rejected the application to abandon its construction.

The story starts in the 1840s with the big railway companies' ambitions to open up the market to Scotland, particularly from London. In 1845 work on the west coast line from Lancaster to Carlisle was started by the company sharing those names (L&C), (which resonates with the last ten years, when work has been done on the same stretch every weekend), while the section northwards from Carlisle had not been started, to be done by the Caledonian Railway. The east coast line was not in place either, as the Tyne and Tweed had not yet been bridged, those completed in 1849 and 1850 respectively, so the Great Northern Railway (GNR) was in on the pantomime also.

This was because although it, the GNR, wanted to connect with "Scotland" via the east coast line eventually, as the route through Yorkshire was shorter and the Leeds and Bradford Railway was already building a track from Shipley to Skipton and Colne, it could see advantages in using the Yorkshire route.

The original route from Yorkshire to connect with the west coast line was the ill-fated Ingleton branch, from Clapham to Low Gill, south of the Tebay gap, at first called the Orton branch. The history of this line is very complex, (see reference at end), and involved many wranglings between several rail companies, but the government was in favour of this line because it was the shortest route, rather than travelling to Lancaster on that newly constructed line and then up to Carlisle.

This line was built by the L&C for a company called the North Western Railway Company (NWR) from 1858 to 1861. If you think our current system of track /station/ rolling stock ownership is crazy, get this, this line was "managed" by two large companies, the London and North Western Railway (LNWR), who had bought the lease from the L&C for their track from Ingleton to Low Gill, and The MR, who had already built an extension of their line from Clapham to Ingleton. They could not agree about the use of the MR's station at Ingleton, so the LNWR built their own on the other side of the Greta Viaduct, and passengers sometimes had to walk over it to continue their journey! The LNWR obviously did not ever want this line to threaten their newly controlled west coast line.

The MR's traffic was therefore being messed about, hence the rationale for it to apply to Parliament, if you're still with me, for the Settle to Carlisle, which was passed in 1866.

No-one was happy with this, particularly the powerful LNWR, who saw their Scottish trade seriously threatened, and in early 1868 they made a favourable offer of their toll for the MR's use of the Ingleton line, pointing out helpfully that it would cost more than two million pounds to build the new (Settle to Carlisle) line, i.e. an awful lot, and a long time to recoup that, if ever. This offer was accepted readily by the MR, but too late; we come back to my second paragraph above and Parliament's rejection of the abandonment of the construction. It should be added that there was a definite fear in Parliament at this time of Railway company amalgamations, which they thought might lead to monopolies, which was obviously a dreaded thing at that time.

There is an alternative view of the MR's cold feet, which is that the economic downturn –read on, it's all happened before–, was the major factor. In May 1866 the leading London discount company Overend, Gurney and Co. suspended payments, which led to a serious financial crisis. The cause has been described as a "Dickensian version of subprime debt", and it was this which caused a shareholder's revolt, a second one; they were obviously a pretty revolting lot, as they didn't want to have the line in the first place.

CONSTRUCTION

It took seven years to build and was the last extant mainline to be built in Britain. It was costed as £2.5 million, but built at £3.5 million. Roughly 6000 men at its peak were employed in its building, with "hundreds" losing their lives, from accidents and the diseases of smallpox, typhus and cholera mainly. There were so many deaths involved in the building of the Ribblehead viaduct that the MR paid for the expansion of the graveyard at St Leonard's church at Chapel-le-dale, where 110 bodies had been added by 1873. Twenty five were buried in Mallerstang.

It is often stated that the line was constructed mainly by hand and dynamite, ensuring a hard life for the navvies (navigators). In fact the latest technology of the time was used, including vertical steam engines, steam lifts, drills and concrete. There were just no mechanical diggers.

Most of the navvies were immigrants, mainly Irish. At Ribblehead they lived in great shanty towns you may have read about on the boards underneath as you passed, with brickworks, several railway lines to quarries as well as the temporary dwellings. No imagination is needed to work out how living here must have been in this wet and exposed place at nearly 1000 feet above sea level.

There were particular problems with constr-uction at certain places, e.g. at Ribblehead, where the twenty four pillared viaduct built on marshy ground meant that each pier had to be set in concrete 25 feet below ground level.

Going north from here the Blea Moor tunnel is 2600 yards long and 500 feet below ground, the only blessing here being that there would be some respite from the frequent foul weather in this area. It took five years to dig, and the rock was winched up seven shafts sunk from above, and deposited in mounds, clearly seen from our route up Whernside. Three of the shafts remain for ventilation.

Ribblehead Viaduct

At Dandry Mire near the head of Garsdale the plan was for an embankment, but after two years of tipping into a never-ending abyss they gave up and built a viaduct, which can't have been much easier.

Dent Head Viaduct

The MR wanted a fast line, in contrast to the Ingleton line, which took one hour and ten minutes for its meagre 22 miles. It in fact turned out to be two miles longer to Carlisle than via Ingleton and Tebay, so to compensate, the design was for high speed, cutting out bends and with less severe gradients than the one in 75 of the LNWR line over Shap Fell. The maximum gradient was therefore fixed at one in 100. The route follows the valleys of the Eden and Ribble upwards from each end and is joined in the middle by a high level section of ten miles. This necessarily means that the 16 miles from Settle to Blea Moor was all at 1 in 100, called "the long drag", although it climbed further to the highest point at Aisgill in Mallerstang, 1169 feet above sea level. This is the highest point that mainline trains get up to in England. To "feed" the poor steam engines and to save time, a long water trough was built in the middle of the lines approaching Garsdale Station, steam heated to prevent icing in winter, so the express trains could take on water without stopping.

Thus it was not built primarily to serve the local communities, Dent station being four miles and a hefty 600 feet ascent away from Dent, and Kirkby Stephen is a mile and a half from the station.

The Midland wanted a distinctive identity for its buildings, the "Derby Gothic," after its headquarters, and already had grand stations at Derby and St Pancras. The stations were therefore built in a common style in three sizes, the largest being for Settle, Kirkby Stephen and Appleby. Unusually you can only access the stations from the platforms, not from the roads. Local stone was used for building; red sandstone for the Eden valley, brick at Appleby, and millstone grit and limestone from Kirkby Stephen southwards. You will also notice the characteristic Midland diagonal fencing.

Arten Gill Viaduct, Whernside beyond

OPERATION

The line opened to passengers in February 1876, and was an immediate success in terms of custom, (to say it was an immediate commercial success cannot be so, costing £3.5 million!) as superior comfort was provided compared with the other lines/companies, which it had to provide to compete with the faster services, and it was heavily advertised as the most interesting route to Scotland, which was probably true.

On opening, the line took three trains a day each way from London to Edinburgh and Glasgow, the fastest time being ten and a half hours to Edinburgh, compared with ten hours ten minutes for the LNWR route and nine and a half by the Great Northern.

A welcome secondary earner for the MR was freight, and several large Lineside Quarries and mines opened as a result of the line, e.g. the Stainforth Lime Quarry, opening in 1873; the Gypsum mine at Kirkby Thore, which is still operating and also imports gypsum, a by-product of de-sulphurisation from Drax power station in Yorkshire, to end up with raw plaster; and also a sawmill in the Eden valley exporting pit props. Currently the freight is mainly coal from Hunterston coal terminal on the Ayrshire coast to the Drax power station in Yorkshire.

In 1923 the Midland merged with the LNWR to form the London Midland and Scottish Railway, and although the new company concentrated on the Shap route, there were still thrice daily fast return trains over the line.

When the railways were nationalised in 1948 the Line was regarded as a duplicate and effectively run down, so that by 1963, when the notorious Dr

The 19:29 arriving at Dent Station from Settle, on a busy midsummer evening

Beeching had plans to close the line for passenger services, which were fortunately shelved, only Settle and Appleby stations remained open. British Rail continued to want the line closed, stating the cost of maintenance, particulary of the Ribblehead Viaduct as the main reason, and as the West Coast Main Line was electrified in 1975 most freight went on that line.

In the 1980s this came to a head, and in 1981 a protest group, the Friends of Settle to Carlisle Line (FoSCL) became active, before the closure notices were posted in 1984. Local Authorities joined with the FoSCL and caused an outcry, discovering a "dirty tricks" campaign by British Rail, i.e. exaggerating the cost of repairs for the line, diverting traffic from the line, and the deployment of their most run down and filthy coaches and locomotives.

Now I was struggling on my bicycle up the start of the Coal Road from Garsdale to Dent station one Saturday in April 2009, training for the Etape Du Dales cycle event, this climb being its most severe, when I came across dozens of folk walking up to Garsdale Station. Normally this road is deserted on this side of the hill. Travelling slowly, I could ask what was afoot, and the answer was that a bronze statue of a dog was being unveiled near the station!

It turned out that the dog, Ruswarp, pronounced "russup", was

the only one to put his paw print to the FoSCL petition against closure. This was not the only reason why he was being immortalised; it was because his master was Graham Nuttall, the first secretary of the Friends of the Settle to Carlisle Line, who unfortunately died in

Ruswarp, Garsdale Station

the Welsh Hills in January 1990, Ruswarp staying with his master's body till early April, when he was found, alive, but did not survive much longer. Graham's favourite spot on the Line was Garsdale.

Two initiatives were to demonstrate that the line was a viable commercial enterprise; the DalesRail, a charter service for ramblers at the weekends, and the Dalesman service following that.

DalesRail was the idea of Colin Speakman, a Leeds teacher, and his friends, who persuaded the Ramblers association to charter the first train to stop at the Dales National Park stations in late summer 1974, 500 ramblers making that first trip a resounding success. Further negotiations led to a scheduled service starting in May 1975, from the Yorkshire towns to the National Park stations plus Kirkby Stephen and Appleby, with two trains on Saturday and one on Sunday, with the latter connecting with a bus service to Swaledale. In 1976 services were extended to and from Carlisle and three Eden valley stations were opened at the weekends. By 1977 the three year experiment was pronounced a definite success, with Kirkby Stephen being the most popular destination, followed by Garsdale and then Dent.

The Dalesman service, a local daily stopping service at eight further stations in the Dales and the Eden valley, had its first outing on the 14th July 1986. There were two return trains on weekdays and one on Saturday. This venture was the work of (mainly) the Settle-Carlisle Joint Action Committee, Cumbria County Council and Ron Cotton, an interesting British Rail man, said to have been moved in 1983 to milk the Settle-Carlisle for all it was worth before closure. The "Saver" ticket brought in for BR in 1980 to counter the results of deregulation of long distance coach services, was his idea. Clearly he, although maintaining loyal to the BR line, couldn't help doing what he was good at, marketing, and by means of such ploys as the £5 maximum fare for Leeds bound travellers and a £1 early bird return from

Skipton to Appleby, he had presided over an increased in revenue of 80% in 1984 over 1982. The truth was that he had found that the Settle to Carlisle was a line of immense potential, disgracefully undersold for years. He retired in 1987, and it is worth quoting his thoughts on rail

Garsdale Station

travel, - "My philosophy was the people's railway. What we needed was mass movement. The opposing forces believed in high quality and high prices…"

Eventually, by 1989, consent by the government to close the line (murder) was refused, thus saving it for the second time, the first one being 120 years before (termination of pregnancy)!

Central to British Rail's exaggerated maintenance claims was the Ribblehead Viaduct, which it claimed in 1983 would cost £7million to replace. Around that time a trial repair to one of the arches revealed that the damage was not terminal, and so in 1989, after the threat of closure had been lifted, it was repaired during a two week closure of the line at the final cost after further work on the piers of around £2million, half of which was promised by English Heritage. The cause was found after removal of the single track (it had been singled in 1985 to reduce outward forces), and ballast. There were a series of six inch square holes in the decking, which is in effect the "roof" of the structure. These had seen wooden scaffold poles poking through, and the decking had been laid round them. When the laying had finished the poles must have been sawed off flush, and when the wood inevitably rotted there was free access for water to the piers, leaching out the limestone mortar and waterlogging the structure, upon which frost could further wreak its damage. Shoddy Victorian work!

Currently, the line is busier than at any previous time, increasingly used by freight as mentioned above, and as a diversion when the West Coast Main Line is closed at weekends for maintenance or in emergencies, although the trains have to swap engines to be pulled by diesel ones.

Well that's it, when you return to Settle hopefully after seeing the sights on the way, have a good onward journey, although it will never be as good as the Settle to Carlisle.

Stations and features on your trip from Carlisle (Open stations in capitals)

CARLISLE

Scotby

Cumwhinton

Cotehill
> Cotehill/Knot Hill tunnel 91 yards
> Drybeck Viaduct 39 yards

ARMATHWAITE
> Armathwaite Viaduct 176 yards
> Armathwaite tunnel 325 yards
> Baronwood tunnels 251 and 207 yards

LAZONBY and KIRKOSWALD
> Lazonby tunnel 99 yards
> Eden Lacy/river Eden Viaduct 137 yards

Little Salkeld
> Little Salkeld Viaduct 134 yards

LANGWATHBY
> Wastebank tunnel 164 yards, 400 yards before: Culgaith tunnel 661 yards

Culgaith
> Crowdundle beck Viaduct 86 yards

Newbiggin
>British Gypsum works, Kirkby Thore

Long Marton
>Long Marton Viaduct 180 yards

APPLEBY
>Ormside Viaduct, River Eden, 200 yards

Great Ormside
>Helm tunnel 571 yards
>
>Griseburn beck Viaduct 142 yards

Crosby Garrett
>Crosby Garrett Viaduct 110 yards
>
>Crosby Garrett tunnel 181 yards
>
>Smardale Viaduct, Scandal Beck 237 yards

KIRKBY STEPHEN
>Birkett Common Tunnel 424 yards
>
>Ais Gill Viaduct 87 yards
>
>Shotlock tunnel 106 yards
>
>Lunds viaduct 103 yards
>
>Moorcok tunnel 99 yards
>
>Moorcock/Dandrymire Viaduct 227 yards

GARSDALE
>Rise Hill Tunnel 1213 yards

DENT
>Arten Gill Viaduct 220 yards
>
>Dent head Viaduct 199 yards
>
>Blea Moor Tunnel 2629 yards
>
>Ribblehead Viaduct 440 yards

RIBBLEHEAD

HORTON-IN-RIBBLESDALE
>Stainforth tunnel 120 yards
>
>X2 short viaducts

SETTLE

Further Reading
(In order of the walk)

Walks in Limestone Country. A. Wainwright (2003) Frances Lincoln.

Walking the Dales. Mike Harding. (1989) Mermaid Books.

The Land of the Lune. John Self (2008) Drakkar Press Ltd.

Walks on the Howgill Fells and adjoining Fells. A.Wainwright (2003) Frances Lincoln.

A pictorial guide to the Lakeland Fells, Book Two, The Far Eastern Fells. 2nd (revised) edition. A.Wainwright, edited Chris Jesty (2005) Frances Lincoln.

A pictorial guide to the Lakeland Fells, Book One, The Eastern Fells. 2nd (revised edition.) A.Wainwright, edited Chris Jesty (2005) Frances Lincoln.

A pictorial guide to the Lakeland Fells, Book Five, The Northern Fells. 2nd (revised edition) A.Wainwright edited Chris Jesty (2008) Frances Lincoln.

Complete Lakeland Fells. Bill Birkett (1994) Harper Collins.

Great British Ridge Walks. Bill Birkett (1999) David & Charles.

Cumbria Way. Paul Hannon (2005) Hillside.

The Ingleton Branch. A lost Route to Scotland. Robert Western (1990) The Oakwood Press.

The Line that refused to Die. Stan Abbott & Alan Whitehouse (1994) The Leading Edge.

Iron Roads North of Leeds. Michael Pearson (2004) Wayzgoose.